Fun Gardening for Kids
30 creative outdoor projects

Fun Gardening for Kids
30 creative outdoor projects

Imaginative ideas for great garden activities for 5–12 year
olds, shown in 500 fantastic step-by-step pictures

Jenny Hendy

southwater

This edition is published by Southwater,
an imprint of Anness Publishing Ltd,
Blaby Road, Wigston,
Leicestershire LE18 4SE
info@anness.com
www.southwaterbooks.com; www.annesspublishing.com

If you like the images in this book and would like
to investigate using them for publishing, promotions
or advertising, please visit our website
www.practicalpictures.com for more information.

Publisher: Joanna Lorenz
Senior Editors: Lucy Doncaster and Emma Clegg
Designer: Lisa Tai
Photographer: Howard Rice
Models: Aidan, Alyson, Anna, Ashley, Christian, Eleanor, Grace,
Holly, Imogen, Jenny, Jessica, Juliet, Kirsty, Lorna, Lucy D., Lucy I.,
Lucy P., Matthew R., Matthew T., Michael, Rhys, Siani and Viv
Production Controller: Steve Lang

© Anness Publishing Ltd 2012

A CIP catalogue record for this book is available from the
British Library.

Previously published as part of a larger volume, *The Ultimate
Step-by-Step Kid's First Gardening Book*

Ethical trading policy

At Anness Publishing we believe that business should be
conducted in an ethical and ecologically sustainable way,
with respect for the environment and a proper regard to the
replacement of the natural resources we employ.

As a publisher, we use a lot of wood pulp in high-quality
paper for printing, and that wood commonly comes from spruce
trees. We are therefore currently growing more than 750,000 trees
in three Scottish forest plantations: Berrymoss (130 hectares/
320 acres), West Touxhill (125 hectares/305 acres) and Deveron
Forest (75 hectares/185 acres). The forests we manage contain
more than 3.5 times the number of trees employed each year in
making paper for the books we manufacture.

Because of this ongoing ecological investment programme,
you, as our customer, can have the pleasure and reassurance of
knowing that a tree is being cultivated on your behalf to naturally
replace the materials used to make the book you are holding.

Our forestry programme is run in accordance with the UK
Woodland Assurance Scheme (UKWAS) and will be certified by
the internationally recognized Forest Stewardship Council (FSC).
The FSC is a non-government organization dedicated to
promoting responsible management of the world's forests.
Certification ensures forests are managed in an environmentally
sustainable and socially responsible way. For further information
about this scheme, go to www.annesspublishing.com/trees

Publisher's note

Although the advice and information in this book are believed
to be accurate and true at the time of going to press, neither the
authors nor the publisher can accept any legal responsibility or
liability for any errors or omissions that may have been made nor
for any inaccuracies nor for any loss, harm or injury that comes
about from following instructions or advice in this book. All
children need to work with adult guidance and supervision
and it is the parent's or carer's responsibility to ensure the
child is working safely.

Contents

Garden entertainment

Even without trees to climb there are more possibilities for adventure in a garden than indoors and, with a little guidance, some basic equipment and a few plants, kids can transform even the smallest outdoor space into a blooming oasis they can be proud of.

► *It's really satisfying picking bright flowers that you have grown in the garden.*

The great outdoors

Green spaces represent freedom – the chance to let off steam, to play more physical and rambunctious games and to simply become carefree. Games created in open air tend to be different to those played indoors, partly because the fluctuating environment stimulates imaginations. The seasons, weather and daily pattern of light and dark affect plants and creatures in many tangible ways and help us to mark the passage of time naturally.

It is a sad fact, however, that kids can be more or less oblivious to such things without direction from adults. Many are reluctant to leave the comfort of the sofa, or to break away from their favourite TV programme or computer game to venture outdoors, especially in cold or damp weather. Entice them out with one of the many projects in this book and be prepared to join in and offer plenty of help and encouragement! Consider giving children their own plot or pots too. Not only does this feel like a special treat, it also helps to teach responsibility. With very young ones, however, you'll need to act as backup, doing extra watering and pest control so that the results of their efforts don't disappoint.

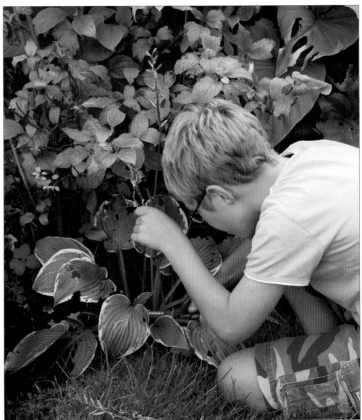

▲ *You can help with all kinds of gardening jobs and maybe even have a patch of your own to tend.*

▲ *Flowers attract a host of insects for nature study.*

▲ *Explore the wonders of nature in your own back yard.*

Designing a children's garden

Having access to a garden can be something of a luxury in urban areas, although a tiny flower- or vegetable-filled balcony can fulfil our basic need to grow food and nurture nature, even in the middle of a city. There are many kinds of garden, large and small, formal and informal, wild or manicured, and some styles and layouts are undoubtedly better suited to the needs of children. Don't worry if your garden is not specifically designed for little ones, however, because any open space where plants are grown has the potential to encourage an interest in gardening and the wild world.

Why should children garden?

Modern living keeps us all indoors for longer than is healthy in terms of body, mind and spirit. Being able to see the sky and experience daylight directly, to breathe in fresh air and to smell flower perfumes or the damp earth after rain, and to become aware of the natural world, all help us to reconnect with nature on a primal level. Modern technology has done nothing to help foster the connection and mobile (cell) phones, personal hi-fis and computer game units should be banned from the garden!

Research has shown that children who are able to play in and explore gardens and green spaces in an unstructured way are better able to remain grounded and in tune with nature as adults. Not surprisingly, this ability helps us to cope better with stress. And children who have positive experiences of gardening and outdoor play and who are encouraged to observe nature often return to these pastimes as adults even after a break of several years.

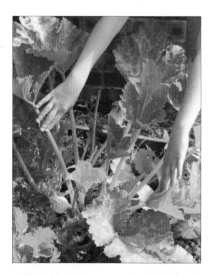

◀ *Plants are fascinating and very beautiful to look at. Investigating inside the long protective leaves of this courgette (zucchini), which has been grown from a small plant, reveals a dramatic yellow flower.*

▼ *There's a whole other world to discover outdoors in your garden. You can help with everyday tasks or take on your own choice of project to bring new interest to your outdoor space.*

ADAPTING A GARDEN FOR CHILDREN

There are plenty of steps you can take to make a garden more child-friendly and stimulating. Try the following where space allows:

✔ Create lots of hidden or secret corners using evergreen shrubs, rigid screens or brushwood or bamboo roll attached to posts or canes (stakes).
✔ Consider making a raised platform or build a boardwalk or walkway to wind through plantings.
✔ Introduce a see-through division using trellis or robust plants, such as bamboo, to protect delicate plantings from an area used for ball games.
✔ Have as large a lawn or open grassy area as you can manage. Sow or turf with a hard-wearing grass or grass/clover mix. Any lawn areas, but especially weedy ones, are good for wildlife too!
✔ If you have room, plant a mini woodland or copse. Set the saplings relatively close together for more instant results and greater potential for play. Silver birch (*Betula pendula*) is ideal.
✔ Leave wild margins or relatively uncultivated areas with long grass, weeds and wild flowers to encourage insects, butterflies and birds.
✔ Grow fruit and vegetables – you don't need a vegetable plot as such, just a few tubs on the patio will suffice. Include fruits that can be picked and eaten straight from the plant, such as tomatoes, raspberries and strawberries.
✔ Grow big, bright colourful blooms – don't worry about colour schemes, especially when the kids are little – as well as larger-than-life foliage plants to tower over children.
✔ Buy a few child-size tools and a small wheelbarrow so that young children can garden alongside you and help move around plants, pots, material for the compost heap etc.

▲ *Create wild areas.*

▲ *Grow fruit and vegetables.*

How to use this book

This book is intended to be used as an inspirational sourcebook by parents and children alike. It is hoped that the projects will act as catalysts, promoting further adventures in gardening and wildlife spotting as kids grow in confidence with their new-found knowledge.

▶ *You will get a kick out of raising plants from seed.*

How to garden

The introductory parts of this book look at how to approach gardening, how to understand some of the common terms and jargon, and how to stay safe, as well as what tools and equipment you will need. This is followed by fascinating facts about plants and soil, with lots of easy mini projects for the junior plant scientist to carry out. We look at how plants grow and what they need to thrive; the seasonal variations; how to control pests and diseases through natural, organic methods, and how to be a 'green' gardener. Gardening really is one of the best ways for children to learn about the cycle of life, to find out where food comes from, and to become aware of the importance of nurturing and supporting the environment.

A wealth of ideas

There then follow five practical chapters that are full of imaginative ideas and colourful activities for 5–10 year olds. There is a chapter on Hands-on Basics, which is devoted to developing good skills when working in the garden, such as taking cuttings, pruning and weeding; Beautiful Blooms, which is all about growing stunning flowers and ideas for presenting them; Growing Things to Eat, an introduction to cultivating fruits, vegetables and

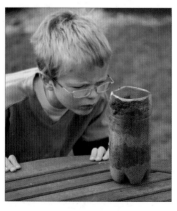

▲ *Have fun experimenting with bugs and worms.*

▲ *Children can help with most garden tasks.*

Gardening safely

Children develop at different rates and only parents or guardians will know when their kids are ready to be introduced to using specific tools or are able to help with certain jobs. Working alongside a grown-up and having a go at something (under close supervision at first) is a great way for children to learn safe practices and to gain the skills needed for greater independence, although continuing adult guidance will be required.

Some of the projects in this book use knives, scissors or garden cutting tools, such as secateurs and pruners, or a saw, hammer and nails. Adult supervision is always required when using these, no matter how old or experienced the child, and more help will be required for younger children. Pictures showing how to do something dangerous, which will require adult help or supervision, have been highlighted with icons, shown below:

(!) the task being shown uses sharp or dangerous implements, such as secateurs, scissors, hammers or spades. Adult help may be required to do the step or, at the very least, supervise children very carefully.

(🖐) the task being shown involves moving or lifting something heavy, using heat or a dangerous substance, or doing something difficult. Adult help may be required to do the step or, at the very least, supervise children very carefully.

herbs; and Wildlife Gardens, which examines ways to encourage and observe all kinds of exciting creatures. In addition, you'll find a section at the end called Plant Profiles that provides really useful information on a whole lot of plants and flowers that will help you garden your way with confidence to green-fingered (green-thumbed) glory!

Choosing a project

When selecting a project, first check the coloured strip across the top of the page to see if it's the right time of year to start the project and how long it might take to make or grow. In order to help you see how easy or difficult a project is, we've also added a star rating system, which works as follows:

★ = the project is 'easy as ABC'. All children from 5 to 12 should be able to tackle these, and there isn't any cutting or specialist tool use involved so it's nice and safe for younger kids. Adult supervision may still be required.

★★ = you should 'give it a try'! There might be some cutting or more manual dexterity involved and children might have to keep tending to the project over a longer period of time. With parental supervision and occasional help, most children will be able to enjoy them.

★★★ = the project is 'nice and challenging'. These are designed for older children and perhaps kids who already have some gardening experience and are ready to try some more advanced techniques. Adult supervision will still always be required for any steps involving dangerous implements.

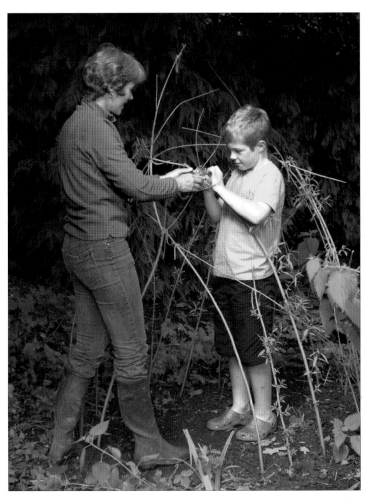

▲ Gardening and exploring alongside an adult is the best way to teach children safety in the garden and further afield.

Getting organized

It's worth reading the brief introduction to the projects, which shows you what you can achieve. So that you know you have everything to hand, use the 'you will need' list to draw all the materials together. There is also a separate 'plant list' with common and Latin names, making it easier to shop for plants or seeds.

▲ Choose a project suitable for the age of your child.

▲ Try propagating plants yourself to save money.

You may already have most things needed for the projects and, if not, the materials specified are often inexpensive and easy to obtain. Many can be sourced from recycled items. You might also consider substituting bits and pieces of equipment with similar elements already in your supplies. And, rather than buying all the plants for a scheme, why not work with the children to see what seedlings, cuttings and divisions might be grown to prepare for planting later in the season or next year? It is both fun and economical.

Preparing to garden!

After ensuring that the garden is as risk-free as it can reasonably be, children should have as much freedom within its boundaries as possible. Dig out plenty of old clothes so that they can run around and get as mucky as they like. The following pages cover the essentials of preparing your young gardeners or wildlife explorers for outdoor fun and helping them stay safe and secure.

Playing safe

Compared to the great outdoors, gardens represent a relatively safe haven for children. There are a few things that you can do to lessen the risk of accidents. Make preparing to garden or play outdoors a simple routine with easy-to-follow rules and boundaries.

▶ It is important to wear sensible clothes when you are gardening.

Safety first
reducing risk in the garden

Before you allow children to roam free in a garden, you need to carry out a basic risk assessment, especially when moving to a new house:

- ✘ Never leave young children unattended in the garden.
- ✔ Look for open or poorly secured manhole or cellar covers (or crawl-space entries) and make sure they are secure before letting children out.
- ✔ Check that all boundaries are impenetrable and gates are locked.
- ✔ Where young children, including friends of your own kids, are likely to use the garden, securely fence off or drain ponds.
- ✔ Look out for sharp objects, including barbed wire, around the garden boundary and consider removing or relocating plants with sword-like leaves (e.g. yucca, agave) as well as prickly or thorny plants, such as roses and barberry (*Berberis* spp.).
- ✔ Make sure your family is up to date with their tetanus immunizations because even a small cut or thorn prick can introduce the disease.
- ✔ Put tops on canes (stakes) to protect eyes.
- ✔ Children love to climb so secure steep drops, such as those next to decks, retaining walls and steps, with guardrails.
- ✔ Lock away tools as well as chemicals, including outdoor paints and preservatives, lawnmower fuel, oils, lubricants and fertilizers.
- ✔ If there are pets around, check the garden for any faeces and pick it up and dispose of it on a regular basis. Stress to children that they must not touch it, and always ensure they wash their hands as soon as they come in.

Local knowledge

Talk to your children about any specific local hazards that may come into the garden from the outside. These might include aggressive ant species, wasp or hornet nests, snakes and other poisonous or biting creatures as well as wild and cultivated plants that can sting or potentially cause allergic reactions. If these could be a problem, adults should be extra vigilant with their supervision.

Summer sun

Children are particularly vulnerable to damage from the sun, especially those with fair or freckly skin, or with blonde or red hair. The results of sunburn are not only painful but can also potentially store up health problems for later life.

1 Apply specially formulated children's sunscreens with a high UVA and UVB protection. Reapply often and limit the amount of time spent in midday sun.
2 Provide shaded rest areas under trees, in tents or under temporary canopies. Offer drinks to keep kids hydrated.
3 Put on a brimmed hat. Boys will often be reluctant but could be persuaded with a cowboy stetson, Indiana Jones-style explorer's hat or pirate's tricorn.
4 Cover up with a T-shirt or long-sleeved shirt.

▲ Long-sleeved T-shirts help protect skin from the sun.

▲ Make sure you wear a sunhat to protect your face.

Safety first
poisonous and irritant plants

Most plants used in this book are safe to handle, unless consumed. If you suspect your child has eaten something poisonous, take them straight to the hospital emergency department with a sample of the plant. Don't try to make them vomit. Never grow *Ricinus communis* (castor oil plant) in a garden used by children as it is highly toxic. Some plants have potentially irritant hairs, or sap that may react with sunlight, and may irritate skin. *Ruta graveolens* (rue) is one of the worst examples of the latter type and contact can require emergency medical treatment.

The list below doesn't include wild plants or mushrooms/toadstools, whose dangers children should also be made aware of. Neither is it comprehensive, so if you are unsure, check first.

- **Angel's trumpets**
  Brugmansia spp. and cvs.
- **Castor oil plant**
  Ricinus communis
- **Cherry laurel**
  Prunus laurocerasus
- **Daffodil** (may irritate skin)
  Narcissus
- **Delphinium**
- **Foxglove**
  Digitalis
- **Ivy**
  Hedera spp.
- **Laburnum**
  Laburnum anagyroides
- **Lily of the valley**
  Convallaria majalis
- **Mezereon**
  Daphne mezereum
- **Monkshood**
  Aconitum
- **Portugal laurel**
  Prunus lusitanica
- **Rhubarb**
  (toxic leaves)
  Rheum raponticum
- **Rue** (may irritate skin)
  Ruta graveolens
- **Spurge** (may irritate skin)
  Euphorbia
- **Tobacco plant**
  Nicotiana
- **Yew**
  Taxus baccata

▲ *Rue can irritate skin.*

▲ *Castor oil plant is toxic.*

Hands and feet

Where possible children should be encouraged to garden without gloves as this increases their sensory experience. However, when using digging or cutting tools or handling prickly or irritant plants, they should put on a pair of children's gardening gloves. Ask your children to wash their hands when they come in from the garden, especially before eating, and discourage nail biting or finger licking when outdoors.

Wellington (rubber) boots or stout shoes protect toes from accidents with tools or sharp objects in the soil, so should always be worn when gardening.

Safety first
using tools and equipment

Showing children how to use tools properly helps prevent accidents and makes gardening more rewarding. Encourage them to clean, tidy away or hang up their garden tools and equipment after use, so they are out of the way and will last longer.

- ✔ Wear thick gardening gloves when using digging or cutting tools. Adult supervision is always required when using these tools.
- ✔ Distribute the load in a wheelbarrow evenly.
- ✘ Don't overload wheelbarrows or garden trolleys, and use one that is a suitable size.
- ✘ Don't try to lift too much soil on a fork or spade when digging. Adult supervision is required, and help should be given.
- ✘ Don't use secateurs or pruners unsupervised and always leave them closed with the safety catch on. Younger children should not use them.
- ✘ Never leave rakes, hoes or other long-handled tools lying on the ground.

▲ *Put away tools.*

▲ *Take care when digging.*

Useful gardening words

When you first start gardening some of the words and phrases you'll hear may sound rather confusing. Don't be put off though. We've explained some of the more commonly used terms for you here, and any that aren't listed will be in the dictionary or on the internet.

▶ *You will already know some gardening terms, but not others.*

Annual This is a plant that grows from seed, flowers, makes more seed and then dies, all in one year. 'Hardy annuals' are easy to grow from seed sown straight in the ground and 'half-hardy' annuals, which need extra warmth to germinate and grow in spring, can't be planted outdoors until the risk of frosty weather has passed. Usually this is early summer.

Bulb This is an underground swelling at the base of a plant's stem that stores food as well as a tiny flowering plant, ready to bloom in the following year.

Chitting In this method for encouraging seed potatoes to start growing, you place them in a light place with their 'eyes' or buds uppermost and allow them to sprout. This is called chitting.

Compost Used frequently in the garden, compost is the dark brown, crumbly rotted-down remains of plant material that is worked into the ground to improve the soil and help grow bigger, better flowers, fruits and vegetables. Compost also describes the bags of potting soil (soil mix) bought to fill pots and baskets.

Crock This is a piece of broken clay pot or tile put into the bottom of a planting container to cover the drainage hole(s) so that soil doesn't block them. You can also use stones or broken-up Styrofoam plant trays.

Cutting A shoot tip, piece of stem or sometimes the root of a plant, cuttings are put into pots or trays of compost (soil mix), or, for easy plants, jars of water. With luck, these pieces make new roots and eventually a whole new plant develops.

Deadheading This is the action of removing old or fading flowers by cutting or pinching them off with thumb and index finger, to prevent the plant from making seeds. Annual plants may stop flowering altogether if allowed to form seed-heads and most plants look better with old flowers removed.

Deciduous This term describes shrubs, trees and climbers that lose their leaves in autumn and grow fresh leaves in spring.

Evergreen Trees, shrubs, climbers and perennial plants that keep their leaves even through the colder winter months are called evergreens.

Fertilizer Another word for plant food, fertilizer comes in different forms, ranging from well-rotted manure to granular or liquid feeds.

Germination When a seed swells with water and starts to grow into a baby plant, unfolding its seed leaves and pushing out its root, this is called

▲ *Sweet peas are beautiful, scented annual plants.*

▲ *Bulbs are little time capsules containing sleeping plants.*

▲ *Compost is made from rotted-down plant waste.*

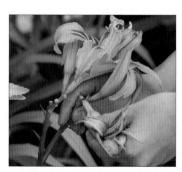

▲ *Deadheading flowers keeps them looking fresh.*

▲ *Use a cold frame as part of the hardening off process.*

▲ *Prick out seedlings when large enough to handle.*

▲ *Perennial plants, such as catmint, come up every year.*

▲ *Pollination is carried out by insects, such as bumble-bees.*

germination. You can see germination in action when you put bean seeds or sprinklings of cress seed on damp blotting paper (*see page 28*).

Hardening off The shoots or leaves of young plants grown from seeds or cuttings indoors or in the greenhouse are too soft at first to be planted straight out in the garden. They must be gradually introduced to cooler outdoor temperatures, stronger light levels and breezier conditions in order to toughen them up. This process is called hardening off and takes two to three weeks. A glass or plastic **cold frame** is often used as a halfway house. Lightly shaded at first, the lid or vents are raised by increasing amounts in the day but are closed at night.

Manure Usually cow or horse dung mixed with straw bedding, this is left to rot down to make garden fertilizer. It's also a great soil improver and mulch. The heap takes about three to four years to break down.

Mulch A thick layer of material, such as chipped tree bark, put on to the soil around plants to help smother weeds. Mulches, such as well-rotted manure or garden compost, also help to keep soils, such as sandy loams, from drying out in summer and these types also provide plant fertilizers.

Naturalize Particularly important for the wild garden look, naturalizing is where certain bulbs or perennials that spread and multiply easily are planted to form large, natural-looking patches in lawns, long grass or the ground under trees.

Perennial This term describes non-woody flowering or foliage plants that are evergreen or more usually **herbaceous**, i.e. they die down in winter and regrow from ground level in spring. The hardy herbaceous perennials as a group contain most of the common border flowers.

Pinching out Carefully nipping off the shoot tip or growing point of a plant, often a seedling or young plant, is called pinching out. It encourages the plant to produce side shoots and become more bushy.

Plunging This is an easy way of thoroughly wetting the roots of a potted specimen before planting. Fill a bucket of water and hold the plant pot under the water surface until the air bubbles stop.

Pollination Bees and other insects transfer male pollen to the female part of the flower – a process called pollination. This allows seed to be produced and fruits to ripen.

Pricking out (Potting on) When a tray of seedlings starts to grow their first set of true leaves and are large enough to handle, each baby plant is moved to another container to give them more room to grow. This is called pricking out. The seedlings are delicate and the tiny roots should be lifted out of the compost (soil mix) or cuttings (seed-starting) mix with the end of a pencil or stick while holding a leaf for support.

Propagation This technique makes more plants and includes several methods, such as sowing seed, taking cuttings, divisions or rooting offshoots or runners. Seeds and cuttings may be put in a **propagator**, which keeps the compost (soil mix) or cuttings (seed-starting) mix warm and moist to encourage germination or rooting.

Pruning Cutting off parts of a woody plant, such as a shrub or climber, to improve its shape, get rid of diseased or damaged stems and branches, or to encourage flowering and fruiting, is called pruning.

Staking This involves using a stick or bamboo cane to prop up a plant and prevent it being damaged by wind or rain or falling over because it is top-heavy.

Tools and equipment

You can now find quite a wide range of gardening tools especially designed to suit the height and body size of younger gardeners. They aren't as heavy as tools for grown-ups and some have adjustable handles so that you can keep using them as you grow.

▶ Pick tools that are just the right size for you to use.

Trowel

One of the most important tools in any garden, a trowel is a mini hand-held spade that is used for making small holes and digging up weeds. They come in various sizes, so make sure you choose one that fits comfortably in your hand and is not too heavy for you to use. They need to be sturdy enough to handle a bit of digging. Take care when using.

▲ Trowel

Hand fork

There are two main types of hand fork: angled ones and flat ones. The angled type is best for loosening the soil between plants in small flower-beds and in window boxes. This makes it easier to sow seeds or plant seedlings, and to pull up any smaller annual weeds that grow between established plants. The flat fork is best for lifting up bigger weeds, complete with their roots, once you have loosened the ground. Take care when using.

▲ Flat and angled hand fork

Gardening scissors

Like normal scissors, gardening scissors can be used for all kinds of tasks in the garden, from cutting string and twine to length and opening seed packets to snipping off dead flower-heads and tidying up straggly plants. They are safer than secateurs (pruners), although they will not cut through thicker twigs or branches in the same way, so you may need to use secateurs sometimes with adult supervision. Take care when using them and never leave them lying open on a surface or the ground. Adult supervision is required.

▲ Gardening scissors

Dibber

Used for making a deep hole in which to plant a seedling, or to make drills or furrows (long, shallow grooves) for sowing rows of seeds, a dibber (dibble) is a useful, but not essential, tool. If you don't have one, you can use a thick stick instead. Take care when using.

▶ Dibber

Plant labels

It is useful to mark where you've sown seeds or planted bulbs in the border, and sowings in pots and trays should always be labelled with the plant name and date. On bigger labels you could also add notes to yourself saying how often plants need feeding or when to harvest. There are fun labels to buy, or make your own from old lolly (popsicle) sticks or strips of plastic cut from clean yogurt containers.

▲ Plant labels

Garden twine

Thicker and softer than normal string, garden twine is used for tying sticks together, for attaching plants to supports or for marking straight lines for sowing. ▲ Garden twine

Gloves

Use these to protect your hands from thorns, wood splinters and stinging nettles and to keep them clean when doing a really mucky garden job. Try to find a pair that fits properly – if they are too big they can be difficult to work in. Some types are thicker for thorn protection and others have rubber grips on the palms.

▲ Gloves

Bucket

Having a bucket to hand is very useful. They are great for plunging plants to wet the roots before planting, collecting clippings, carrying soil and compost and even for transporting hand tools. There are many sizes, but do not overfill a larger one or it may be too heavy to carry.

▲ *Bucket*

Hoe

A long-handled piece of equipment, a hoe or cultivator is useful for weeding and breaking up the soil surface ready for sowing. It slices like a knife under the roots of weeds, which then shrivel up and die in dry weather and can easily be pulled up. Because the hoe has a long handle, you don't have to bend down to weed, so no backache! Like spades, hoes have a sharp cutting edge, so you must always ask an adult to supervise and take great care when using.

◀ *Standard rake*   ▶ *Hoe*

Watering can

An essential piece of equipment for watering and feeding, try to get a can with a handle at the side and the top, since this will help you handle it and put water where it is needed. Ones with a 'rose' or sprinkler fitting on the end are best for watering delicate seedlings and young plants. Take it off to water the base of a plant, under the leaves. Do not overfill or it may be too heavy to carry.

▲ *Watering can*

Rakes

There are two types of rakes: standard soil rakes and spider (leaf) or spring tine rakes. Soil rakes have rigid prongs set at a right angle to the handle. They are used for loosening and levelling out soil. Spring tine rakes have much thinner prongs that fan out from the end of the handle. These are used for gathering leaves or small bits of twig from lawns. Never leave rakes or other long-handled tools lying on the ground. Adult supervision is required.

▶ *Spade*

Spade

Used for digging big holes or for turning over the soil to mix in compost or manure, spades are one of the most useful pieces of equipment. Try to get one that is not too tall for you, or you will find it hard to use. Since the edge of the blade is sharp, you must always wear stout shoes or boots. Adult supervision is required and great care should be taken when using one.

Wheelbarrow

Extremely useful for transporting tools, compost and plants around the garden, wheelbarrows are available in several sizes. Use one that is the correct size for you, and never overload it. They can be heavy, so adult supervision is required and you may need to ask for help.

▲ *Spider rake*

◀ *Wheelbarrow*

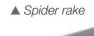

Warning!

Adult supervision is always required when children are using sharp or potentially dangerous implements, such as garden forks. Adult help may also be required for any lifting or moving anything heavy. Children should not use saws, hammers, drills or other electrical garden equipment. It is up to the parent or carer to ensure the child is working safely.

tools and equipment   15

The living garden

In this chapter you'll find out how plants work, what they need to thrive and why they are so useful to us. You'll be introduced to the way plants are named and what plant parts are called. Budding scientists will enjoy looking at soil and investigating minibeasts and there are fascinating facts about nature's cycles, the weather and seasons.

Why we need plants

If it wasn't for the green stuff all around us, we simply wouldn't exist. Plants create the air we breathe (oxygen) as a by-product when they use the sun's energy to convert carbon dioxide into sugars. These sugars form the building blocks right at the start of the food chain.

▶ You can grow many plants in all kinds of different containers.

Nature's favourite colour

The leaves and stems of plants contain a green colouring or pigment called chlorophyll. Sometimes it is masked by other colours, such as reds and purples, but it is always there. It allows plants to trap the sun's energy (photons) and use it to split water absorbed from the soil into hydrogen and oxygen. The hydrogen is combined with carbon dioxide, which the plant takes in through special holes in the leaves, and the end result is sugar and oxygen. The sugar is used as the plant's energy source, while the oxygen is released into the atmosphere through the same little holes and we, and other animals, can breathe it in.

Although you can tell from looking at a beautiful green forest or a meadow that there's masses of chlorophyll in plants, you may not realize that seas, lakes and rivers are also full of tiny plants, called algae and phytoplankton. These are some of the most important in the earth's defences, helping to mop up excess carbon dioxide – a potentially harmful greenhouse gas – and stopping the earth from becoming too hot.

Food for all

Plants, like us, need food to survive. Theirs is created in the leaves during an amazing chemical reaction called photosynthesis, when the sugars made from trapped sunlight join together to make other materials including cellulose, a major plant building block, and starch. Starch is a way for plants to store excess sugars for future use. Potato tubers contain a lot of starch.

Everybody can benefit from plants, whether they are eaten directly or by the animals that are then eaten. Cows, for instance, which provide us with meat or milk, eat grass or are fed with grains or seeds that are produced by crops growing in fields. In addition, little water creatures eat algae and phytoplankton and eventually are themselves eaten by fish, which end up on the dinner table.

As well as leafy vegetables, such as lettuce, 'flower' vegetables, such as cauliflower and broccoli, and root vegetables, like carrots, there are all kinds of fruits, seeds, grains and nuts that we can eat. And, for a touch of sweetness, there's sugar from sugar cane or sugar beet; honey, made by bees from the plant nectar they collect, and maple syrup.

▲ Algae produces oxygen and can be eaten by water creatures.

▲ The green colour of leaves is due to chlorophyll.

▲ Cows eat grass and use this food to grow and to make milk, which we can drink.

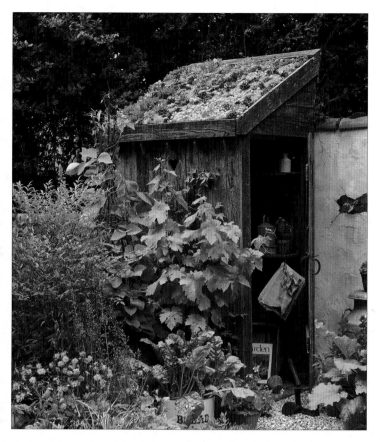

▲ *A green roof such as this creates another habitat for insects and helps keep buildings cool.*

Useful plants

While not all plants are edible (some are poisonous!), man has discovered, often by trial and error, that certain types can help us feel better if we become ill. Many of the medicines we use today are based on chemicals made originally by plants. Some of the common kitchen herbs, such as sage, mint and thyme, now mainly used for flavouring food, have also been used as medicines in the past. Today, you can buy herbal remedies, as well as teas and infusions, such as chamomile and peppermint, from pharmacies, health-food shops and supermarkets.

Plants are also grown to provide materials for a huge range of things, including dry vegetation, such as straw, sedge and rushes, for building thatched roofs or for weaving. We make clothes from spun cotton, hemp and flax (used for linen). Trees are cut for timber used to build houses and other structures, and wood pulp makes cardboard and paper. Plants that died millions of years ago and that have turned into coal are burnt as fuel to keep us warm or to generate electricity. In the future, plants may be grown to produce biofuels, a renewable energy source used to power cars and machines.

Plants are cool!

In our gardens we use trees and climbers to provide shade, but plants in general help to keep our surroundings cool, especially in towns and cities where concrete, tarmac and brick buildings store and give out a lot of heat. Parks, gardens and tree-lined roads help to make life in urban places more enjoyable, provide shade and do not store heat in the same way as man-made materials. You may also see some buildings being fitted with 'green' roofs planted with grass or drought-resistant plants. Plants act like sponges, absorbing harmful air pollution, soaking up rainfall and helping to prevent flooding. The protective covering of greenery also slows down the wearing away of soil by wind and rain.

Brightening our world

Plants, both indoors and outside, make our world more beautiful and colourful. In addition, when they do take root, all kinds of creatures can move in too. By gardening you can turn a 'desert' balcony, roof terrace or concrete-covered yard into an oasis, lush with aromatic leaves and fragrant flowers and buzzing with insects. Although green is usually the background colour and comes in a great many shades, there's a dazzling array of flower colours and forms to marvel over, as well as two-tone and textured foliage. All the effort you put into a garden or green space is paid back by the wheelbarrow load! You get such a great feeling of achievement from the plants you have nurtured, the pots and beds you have planted, and the fruits, vegetables and herbs you have grown, picked and eaten – and you are also helping the environment.

▲ *Everyone enjoys the fragrance and aroma of plants.*

▲ *Many herbs and plants have medicinal benefits.*

Parts of a plant

There are lots of types of plants. Many have flowers, some have hairy leaves, some are tall and woody, and others creep along the ground. However different they look, they mostly work in a similar way and garden plants usually have a common basic structure.

▶ *If you look closely at plants you will be able to see the different parts.*

The structure of plants

Plants come in a huge range of shapes and sizes. Ones pollinated by insects tend to have similarly structured and quite colourful and showy blooms. Those pollinated by wind are mostly plain without petals as they don't need to do any advertising.

The blanket flower shown below is a typical example of one of the largest plant families, the daisy family. Like most plants it has a **root system**, which supplies the plant with water and nutrients from the soil. These are drawn up the **main stem**, along branches to **leaves** and **flowers**. This species has open-centred blooms but the actual flowers are tiny, without **petals** and are tightly clustered in the central disc. Botanists call these **disc florets**, and the petals **ray florets**. Notice the protective covering of green, leaf-like bracts that encase the flower-buds. These are called **sepals**.

The structure of flowers

Most flowers have male and female parts. Some are able to pollinate themselves, while others need wind or insects to carry the pollen from one flower to another. In order to attract insects, they often have brightly coloured **petals**, which make up the majority of the flower. The centre may be marked with a contrasting 'target' that helps insects home in on the nectar and pollen. The lines are called **nectar guides**.

The reproductive parts of the flower are clustered together. The female part, or **stigma**, which sticks out to receive the male pollen, is usually surrounded by a number of male **stamens**. These stamens are each made up of a stalk (called a **filament**) and the pollen-bearing **anther**. The stigma, its stalk (called a **style**) and the seed-bearing **ovary** at its base make up the female reproductive organs. Together these are called the **carpel**. When the pollen grains land on the sticky stigma, they grow down the style into the ovary. When this happens, pollination takes place and seeds are produced.

PARTS OF A PLANT

disc florets
sepals
flower stem
seed-head
flower
petal (ray floret)
main stem
flower-bud
leaf
root system

PARTS OF A FLOWER

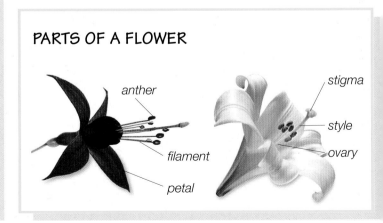

anther
filament
petal
stigma
style
ovary

How plants are named

One of the hardest things about gardening is learning scientific names. Buttercup and daisy are easy to remember, so why bother? Well, the same plant can have many common names but these don't usually tell you much.

▶ All plants have a unique scientific name, and most have a common one.

Unlocking the secret code!

All living things, not just plants, are given a scientific name that helps us to understand the relationships between them. It also means that whoever is talking about the plant or animal, in whatever country, everyone is using the same name and there's no confusion.

The system of naming was invented by the Swedish botanist, Carl Linnaeus in the 18th century. It's mostly based on Latin but Greek is also used. The code can incorporate things such as the name of the person who discovered the particular plant or animal, its country of origin, flower colour, leaf shape and so on. In fact you'll discover there's a lot of useful information in the scientific name once you start decoding!

Genus and species

The first word of the two-part name is the **genus**. This describes a group of plants that are more closely related to each other than to anything else. This can contain a wide range of plants, from trees, shrubs and climbers to herbaceous perennials or annuals. Some of the plants might only be found high up in mountains, while others might live in boggy ground next to a low-lying lake or river.

The second word refers to the **species**. This word identifies all the different plant types that belong in the genus. With some plants, there is only one plant or species in the genus, but in many cases there is more than one. For example, *Prunus persica* is a peach, while *Prunus avium* is a cherry. The first word, *Prunus*, tells you that they belong to the same genus, while the second words, *persica* and *avium*, tell you what species the plant is.

Variations

Subtle differences within a species that occur in nature are described by a third word, which tells you what variety, subspecies or form the particular plant is. If man has artificially created the plant, the variation is called a **cultivar**. The variations are written

---

ALL IN A NAME

The first word in a name tells you what 'genus' the plant belongs to. This can be a big group of plants, or just one.	The second word shows you what 'species' the plant is. This helps you tell the difference between plants in the same genus.

$$\boxed{Prunus} \quad \boxed{persica} \quad \boxed{\text{'Peregrine'}}$$

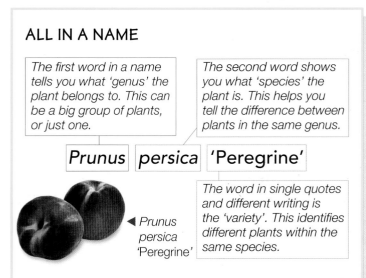

◀ *Prunus persica* 'Peregrine'

The word in single quotes and different writing is the 'variety'. This identifies different plants within the same species.

---

in single quotation marks, so they are easy to spot. For example, a variety of *Prunus persica* is *Prunus persica* 'Bonanza'. Lots of species, such as apples, peaches, potatoes and many others, have many varieties, including names you will recognize, such as 'Granny Smith' or 'Golden Delicious'.

Common names

As well as their scientific names, many plants also have common names, which you may be more familiar with. Some well-known names are 'daisy', 'poppy' or 'lily'. While these are fine for talking about plants in general, you do need to know the scientific names if you want to be more precise. Some plants do not have common names, or if they do then they can also vary from country to country, and there is often more than one name for the same thing, so they can be confusing! For this reason we have given the scientific names as well as the common names (where there is one) in the plant lists and the Plant Profiles section. This means you can buy exactly the right thing, and learn the proper names at the same time. It will also impress your parents!

What is soil?

When you're digging in the dirt or making mud pies, you might not realize how valuable the crumbly brown stuff is. If it wasn't for soil, the earth would be a pretty barren place. Most plants need it to grow into, as few, apart from mosses and lichens, can survive on bare rock.

▶ *Knowing your soil type lets you look after it better.*

Raw materials

Soil is a mixture of finely ground-up rocks, sand and rotted-down plant and animal remains. There are many different soil types named according to how they were formed and where they come from. Basic types include sand, loam or clay, each of which has different properties.

Acid or alkaline?

As well as the different soil types, soil can have a different pH. The pH scale runs from 1 to 14, where 1 is extremely acidic and 14 extremely alkaline. The number 7 is the midway or neutral point. Most garden soils have a pH ranging from slightly above or slightly below neutral. On the vegetable patch

---

WHAT'S YOUR SOIL TYPE?

To work out your soil type, go into the garden and see what it looks like and how it feels.

Sandy soils These types are pale and very free-draining because of the high sand content in them. They are easy to weed and warm up quickly in spring, but can dry out easily.

Loam soils These types of soil are dark and crumbly and usually quite fertile. They contain a mixture of clay and sand as well as lots of rotted plant and animal matter.

Clay soils These types of soil are slow to warm up in spring and in winter are often waterlogged. In summer they can sometimes dry hard like concrete, and crack.

TESTING THE pH OF SOIL

A simple pH testing kit will quickly show you if you have acid, neutral or alkaline soil.

1 Use the end of an old teaspoon to scoop a moist soil sample into the test tube provided with the kit. Carefully break the capsule containing the chemical and pour it on to the soil.

2 Add water to the test tube, following the instructions. Put the stopper in the test tube and, holding firmly between thumb and index finger, give it a really good shake.

3 Leave the contents to settle, then hold the test tube up to the chart provided with the kit and compare the liquid with the chart. Read off the pH value.

MAKE A MINI WORMERY

If you want to study the activities of earthworms for a few days, make this mini wormery. You will be able to see how they pull substances from the surface of the soil down, mixing in beneficial nutrients.

1 Cut the top section off a plastic bottle and ask an adult to make some holes in the base using a skewer. Fill the bottle with alternating layers of washed sand and garden soil enriched with compost.

4 Water the mixture with a watering can. Don't make it too soggy. Replace the top section of the bottle but leave the lid off for ventilation, or the peelings will rot and the worms will suffocate.

2 Very carefully dig up three or four worms from the garden using a trowel, then add them to the top of the soil layer in the mini wormery. They will quickly burrow down out of sight.

5 Stand the wormery in a cool, sheltered place outside, such as in a shady border or under a tree, and loosely cover the whole bottle with black plastic to completely keep out light.

3 Add food in the form of broken-up pieces of potato peelings to the top of the bottle. Don't add too many at once or they will start to rot before the worms can deal with them.

6 After a few days you will see that the worms have pulled the peelings down into the soil. Can you spot any worms? You have to be quick as they don't like light! Release back into the wild when you have finished.

---

you may need to add lime before sowing or planting brassicas, for example. Always pH test your soil before trying to adjust the acidity or alkalinity and never apply lime at the same time as fertilizer or manure.

Some plants can only grow on acidic or lime-free soils. These are known as ericaceous plants and include rhododendrons, azaleas, pieris, camellia and many heathers. Others prefer alkaline or neutral soil, so it is important to work out which type you have.

Teeming with life

Healthy, fertile soil is crammed full of tiny creatures – if you could shrink yourself down to the size of a grain of sand it would seem full of terrifying monsters! As well as these organisms, which are mostly harmless vegetarians living on decaying vegetable matter, there are fungi and bacteria. These last two groups break down plant and animal remains and produce materials that help bind microscopic particles together and convert hard-to-break-down substances into useful plant foodstuffs. Fungi often have a special relationship with particular plants too, helping their seeds to germinate and their roots to grow properly.

At the next size up, there are the invertebrates, meaning animals that don't have a backbone. These include worms, slugs, ants, fly and beetle larvae, mites, centipedes, woodlice, springtails and fungus gnats. Worms are especially important as they are like mobile factories moving through the soil, pulling dead plant material below and mixing plant foods deeper. As they tunnel, they create channels that allow air and water to get down to where the roots need them. The channels also help soils drain and open up the structure so that plant roots can grow more easily.

What plants need

Light, water and food are essential for survival and growth, but different plants need more or less of them. Fitting the right plant to the right spot in the house or garden is part of the skill you will develop as a gardener. You can find helpful information in Plant Profiles.

► *Potted plants need plenty of water and sunshine to thrive.*

Light of life

Wherever they are located, whether in a shady corner of the garden, on a windowsill or on a sunny patio, plants need and use light from the sun to make energy for life (*see 'Nature's favourite colour' on page 18*). Different plants require different amounts of light, however, and if they get too little or too much they can become very unhappy. There are two types of plants: those that love sun and those that like shade.

Sun-loving plants

You can often spot plants that thrive in hot, dry places just by looking at them. The leaves may be thick and fleshy with a waxy coating, storing water inside them. Sometimes though, the leaves are very small and covered in a mealy or flour-like coating, hairs or wool that makes them appear grey or white. This reflects the light, keeping the plant cool and reducing evaporation. Other plants need more moisture and may have large colourful leaves and flowers. In general, plants with purple- or red-tinged leaves and gold variegated kinds need more light than plain green ones.

TURNING HEADS

You may not realize it, but plant stems, leaves and flowers move during the day. You can observe this with pansies, which all turn to face the same direction to get the maximum amount of light. This has an added benefit, as the display attracts passing insects.

1 Fill a pot with potting compost (soil mix) and plant with several pansies. Arrange them so that the flowers are all facing in different directions.

2 Water the plants and stand in a spot in good light. After about a week you will see that the flowers have all turned to face the sun.

▲ *Sun-loving plants, such as lavender, prefer hot, dry spots.*

▲ *Shade plants tend to need more moisture than others.*

Shade-loving plants

These often come from woodland areas and tend to be quieter in colouring than sun lovers, with dark green leaves (maximum chlorophyll) and white, blue, yellow or soft pink flowers more common than red or orange blooms. Leaves may be large, to try to capture as much light as possible and, in the case of ferns, the blades are often finely cut and lacy. Woodland plants thrive in soils full of decayed leaf and plant material that acts like a sponge, keeping water available. The roots may be quite fine and fibrous, so they are not designed for storing water and withstanding drought. If you put a shade-loving plant in full sun, the thin leaves tend to scorch or turn yellow.

Why plants need water

If you have ever seen brown grass or shrivelled flowers during hot weather then you will know that plants become ill-looking and can die if they don't get enough water. This is because it is water that moves minerals and stored food around the plant, as well as keeping the cells, the building blocks of life, the right shape so that they can work properly. Evaporation of water from the leaves also helps to keep the plant cool, in much the same way as sweating cools us down. Water is required right at the start of a plant's life too, to trigger germination, which is when a seed starts to grow a baby plant.

Overwatered plants, on the other hand, are drowning. When the roots are too wet and haven't got enough air, they begin to die and may have trouble taking up nutrients. Very wet weather can cause this problem outside, and it is common in plants in containers that have been given too much water.

It is important, then, that you keep an eye on your plants and feel the soil to see if it is too dry or wet. Wilting leaves are often a sign of thirst and if the soil is dry it's safe to give it a thorough soaking. However, if the soil is damp, it could mean that something has attacked or blocked the roots under the soil surface and the plant simply can't drink the water that's there. If you don't tackle a thirsty plant quickly, it may not recover fully. *See page 26 for watering techniques.*

Signs of overwatering include dropping or drooping leaves and soggy compost (soil mix). You may need to carefully take the plant out of its pot and pat the root-ball with kitchen paper to draw out some excess water. If it is very wet, stand the plant on kitchen paper overnight. Repot the plant, adding extra compost if needed, and keep an eye on it.

How plants drink

The way plants draw up water from the soil is very clever. The action starts in the leaves, which release moisture into the air. The loss of water (**transpiration**) creates a suction through the fine water channels that connect the roots to the leaves and water is drawn up through the stems, rather like the way a drink is pulled up a straw when you suck on it. This process is called **capillarity**. Wind and heat makes plants transpire (lose moisture through the leaves) faster, which means that more water is drawn up and the soil or compost (soil mix) dries out more quickly. In cool or still weather, plants transpire at a slower rate, so plants need less water at their roots.

PLOTTING THE ROUTE OF WATER

Using food dyes and a couple of white flowers (which will show the result most clearly), you can see the movement of water through the stems to the leaves and flowers (capillarity). It may take a day or two, so be patient!

1 Take three tall drinks glasses and three-quarters fill them with water. Divide a sachet of cut flower food between the glasses. This gives the blooms the energy they need to survive without their roots.

2 Add a few drops of coloured food dye so that you end up with one yellow, one red and one blue. Later you can experiment by mixing the colours to make green, purple and orange.

3 Take some white cut flowers, in this case chrysanthemums, and cut the stems at an angle to increase the surface area over which water can be absorbed and ensure they don't have an airlock. Put a flower stem in each glass.

4 Stand the flowers out of direct sunlight, but not in the dark. The flowers should show traces of colour in the petals within two days, showing how the water moved up the stem to the petals.

WAYS TO WATER

There are several ways of watering plants. Potted outdoor ones may need watering at any time of the year.

Misting The air indoors is too dry for some plants. Spray regularly with a hand mister or stand plants on a tray of moist gravel. Don't spray plants with felted leaves, succulents or cacti.

Watering from below Plants with hairy leaves can rot if watered from above. Soak the roots from below by standing in a bowl of tepid water. Water trays of newly sown seed in the same way.

Plunging Always plunge plants in a bucket of water before planting to give them a drenching. Hold the surface of the potting compost (soil mix) under the water and wait for the bubbles to stop.

Directing water Take the rose (sprinkler head) off a watering can to direct the flow under the leaves, where it's needed. Avoid watering overhead as droplets bounce off leaves and are wasted.

Watering with a rose Use a fine rose to water cuttings and seedlings that could be damaged by a strong jet of water. Use a slow sweeping motion, starting away from the pot or tray.

Feed me!

Plants, like us, require food to survive. Rather than cooking and eating things, plants draw up nutrients from the soil through their roots and circulate them via their stems to leaves, buds and, in particular, any new growth, such as buds, shoots or baby leaves. Because they can only get nutrients from the soil, it is important that the earth plants stand in is well fertilized before they are sown or planted to give them a good start in life. They will eventually use up the food, however, which is why you need to add extra fertilizer, especially during the growing season. Plants that are in pots or containers need most attention as they have access to only the compost (soil mix) in the pots, and will use up their supplies more quickly than those in the ground.

Lack of the right foods or nutrients can cause all kinds of visible changes in plants. Leaves may turn red, purple or, most often, yellow and look sickly when starved, but some fungal diseases or stresses, such as too much light and heat or overwatering, can make that happen too. Another sign of starvation is that leaves and flowers get smaller and overall growth looks stunted. Correct the problem by applying diluted liquid feed (fertilizer) to moistened soil or compost, following packet instructions. Keeping a close eye on your plants will help you spot problems early on.

Feeding techniques

Food is available as soluble fertilizer, a powder that needs to be mixed with water before applying; liquid feed, which also needs diluting; granular fertilizer, which can be mixed with compost (soil mix) or sprinkled on the surface; and rotted garden compost or manure, which is dug into soil or used as a mulch.

Feed plants during or just before the growing season. Always follow manufacturer's instructions when applying fertilizers and ask a parent to help if you aren't sure. Giving more than the recommended dose can damage plants. Wear gloves and/or wash your hands after handling fertilizers.

Each packet of fertilizer will have an NPK ratio, which tells you relatively speaking how the three main nutrients (nitrogen, phosphorous and potassium) are balanced. Different plants need an appropriate fertilizer, so always check. For example, tomato food is high in potassium (K) because more potassium is needed for fruits, such as tomatoes, to grow. As well as these main nutrients you will also often see trace elements, such as iron, magnesium and copper, listed in the ingredients. Plants use these in minute amounts.

These are the main nutrients in fertilizer:

Nitrogen This has the chemical symbol N. It is used for new shoots and leaves. Yellowing older leaves may indicate nitrogen deficiency.

Phosphorus This has the chemical symbol P. It is involved in the healthy growth of a plant's roots.

Potassium This has the chemical symbol K. It is essential for flower and fruit production.

▲ *The tomato plant on the left is starving. Its leaves are yellow and it hasn't produced any fruits. The plant on the right has strong, healthy growth with green leaves and plenty of fruits ready to ripen.*

FOOLPROOF FERTILIZERS

It is important to use the correct technique for applying different fertilizers. Always wash your hands afterwards.

Soluble fertilizer This is usually powder or crystals. Use the scoop provided to measure the right amount of feed. Mix thoroughly with water. Follow packet instructions. Wash your hands.

Liquid fertilizers These must be diluted. Use the measuring cap and stir the correct amount into the water using a bamboo cane (stake) or stick. Follow packet instructions. Wash your hands.

Granular fertilizers These are slow-release types. Work into the compost (soil mix) or soil or mix with potting compost (soil mix) before planting. Follow packet instructions. Wash your hands.

Compost and manure Well-rotted garden compost or manure feeds plants and improves the condition of the soil. Fork in during late winter/early spring or spread on the surface as a mulch.

Be a weather monitor

It's fun to keep track of the weather and to record temperatures and rainfall just like meteorologists (people who study weather and climate) do. You can use the information to work out when you might need to carry out gardening activities, such as sowing, harvesting, protecting tender plants or watering pots and containers. If it is going to be very hot, move shade-loving house plants to a spot away from windows, and make sure they get enough water.

To measure the amount of water falling in a day you can use a specially calibrated rainwater gauge, which is pushed into the ground and gives the measurement in millimetres or inches. Hold the gauge perfectly level, with your eye on the water line, to read it accurately. Empty the gauge each day after rain or you will get a false reading.

A garden thermometer measures the temperature in degrees centigrade or fahrenheit. Attach to a wall or post in a sheltered, shaded part of the garden, as direct sun or wind can affect the accuracy of your readings. Some thermometers record both the minimum and maximum daily temperatures.

▲ *Read the rainwater gauge at eye level.*   ▲ *Use a garden thermometer to check daily temperatures.*

Nature's natural cycle

A garden is a wonderful place to observe the cycle of life. Whether you like watching the magic of a seed germinating and growing into a plant, or enjoying the changes in the seasons in the garden, there is always something going on outside!

▶ *It is fun to germinate seeds and watch them grow into little plantlets.*

The story of seeds

The cycle of growth for plants starts with a seed. This may be as small as a poppy seed or as large as a coconut, but the process is exactly the same. Some seeds lie dormant until there are exactly the right conditions – enough moisture and warmth – to trigger germination. This is when the seed swells and a shoot starts to grow. This will keep on growing up towards the light until it pops up above the earth. The plant should then mature and, in time, will produce its own seeds. Many of these may be lost to wind or eaten by animals (incuding us!), but some find their way into the soil and the process begins all over again.

Nature's recycling

Nothing is wasted in the natural world. After plants have died down and leaves have fallen from the trees, their remains rot down and return to the soil. Here they feed and nurture the next round of growth.

A rotten apple is a good example of nature's recycling. When it ripens and falls to the ground it might be fed upon by birds and wasps. Soon, microscopic fungi get to work, breaking down the fruit and releasing substances that butterflies can feed on too. Finally, the fungus itself starts to reproduce. Meanwhile, if the seeds inside the apple survive they may germinate and grow into another apple tree, starting off a new cycle.

FROM SEED TO SHOOT

Seeds must absorb moisture to trigger germination. You can watch this in action when you take a dry, dormant broad (fava) bean and wedge it next to damp blotting paper. It soon activates and bursts into life!

1 Cut a piece of blotting paper to fit inside a large glass jar. Press it against the sides and overlap the edges. Blotting paper is ideal because it is thick enough not to collapse when wet.

2 Fill the space inside with cotton wool balls, then pour in water to a depth of 2cm/¾in. Keep this water topped up but below the bean seeds. Seeds need water plus air to germinate as otherwise they would drown.

3 Take three or four dried broad beans and push them down between the glass and the damp blotting paper, spaced evenly around the jar. The paper should hold the beans in position.

4 Replace the lid to keep humidity high and stand in a light, warm spot. After 5–7 days you will see roots and a green shoot appear. The roots will grow downwards and the shoot will grow upwards and develop leaves.

FROM FLOWER-BUD TO SEED-HEAD

Here you can see how a flower, in this case a viola, transforms from a tightly folded bud to an open bloom ready to be pollinated. After the bee has visited, the flower begins to fade and the seed-head swells. Finally the ripe head bursts, releasing the seed.

THE LIFE CYCLE OF A LEAF

This shows the development of a leaf. It starts with a leaf that has just unfurled from a bud. It continues to grow to full size, then, in autumn, it turns yellow and the shrub reabsorbs all useful substances. The brown remains are then broken down by fungi on the ground.

THE CYCLE OF THE SEASONS

In many countries away from the Equator, each season is different, bringing assorted weather, shorter or longer days and varying temperatures. These all affect the plants in your garden, as well as the rhythm of life.

Winter Short days and long nights along with cold temperatures slow most plant growth down to a full stop. Rain turns to hail, sleet or snow. Evergreen plants, some hardy flowering shrubs, heathers, climbers and a few early flowering bulbs provide scatterings of blossom. Birdbaths need thawing and birds need feeding regularly.

Spring Bulbs are some of the first flowers to appear in early spring, followed by fruit tree blossoms. The newly opened leaves of deciduous trees are bright green. Perennial plants push up and weeds also start to grow. Insects and other creatures slowly come out of hibernation. Birds start to sing again and build nests.

Summer Early summer flowers burst into bloom and the vegetable garden produces its first crops. The days get longer and the temperatures increase. Baskets and patio pots must be watered regularly and birdbaths filled daily as rainfall decreases. Insects multiply and you can hear the buzz of bees at work as they pollinate your plants.

Autumn Days start to get shorter and noticeably chilly. Many plants produce fruits, berries or seed-heads. Birds, mammals and other creatures feast on the bounty, fattening up ready for hibernation or to help them survive the winter. The leaves of deciduous trees and shrubs begin to change colour. Leaves drop and herbaceous perennials die down.

SPRING

WINTER

SUMMER

AUTUMN

Growing with nature

Gardeners can worry a lot about bugs and other creatures nibbling at their prize flowers or vegetables. Though we might be tempted to think a garden belongs solely to us, many insects and animals also make it their home, so we should respect their rights too.

▶ Creepy-crawlies are fascinating to watch and many are beneficial.

Getting a balance

You don't need to use chemicals for every type of pest. For every kind of bad guy there is a predator that feeds on it. Sometimes there will be so many pests that you will notice them on your plants. This is because it can take a little while for the good guys to move in and eat them! But, rather than reaching for the bug killer and risk harming beneficial insects too, it is better to wait a while. With some chemical-free techniques you can grow healthy plants without harming vulnerable creatures such as bumble-bees.

Encouraging the good guys

Although you might be scared of spiders or bees, they are actually extremely helpful and important, so should be encouraged. Here are some of the most beneficial insects and animals for the garden:

Bees Almost all types of bee are under threat. They are vital pollinators. Don't use insecticides or weedkillers. Leave untidy corners with weeds and long grass, and provide nectar plants.

Birds Feeding birds year round and creating habitats (shelters and places to nest) encourages them to stay and forage for insects. Even seed-eating birds feed their young on insects.

Centipedes These are brown, fast-moving hunters with lots of legs that skulk in similar places to ground beetles. Build them a log pile home.

Frogs and toads These amphibians eat flies and slugs. They like the cover of long grass and log piles as well as damp places, such as bog gardens or mini ponds.

Ground beetles These fast-moving predators scurry unseen beneath leaf litter, bark mulch and ground cover plants, where they attack insect pests and slugs at night.

Hoverflies These flies look like small wasps. Their larvae gobble up aphids, and adults are excellent pollinators, so they are a welcome addition to the garden. Provide nectar-rich flowers, especially in white, yellow or orange colours to tempt them.

Lacewings Larvae of these boggle-eyed beauties with green or brown bodies and lacy wings love aphids. *See 'Lacewing Lodge' on page 183.*

Ladybirds (ladybugs) Both the larvae and adults of these spotted beetles munch aphids. An evergreen climber-covered wall will shelter adults over winter.

Spiders Web builders and species that pounce on prey are useful for controlling mosquitoes and gnats.

MAKING A GROUND BEETLE TRAP

If you want a closer look at these beneficial beetles, check this trap each morning, then release them.

1 Dig a hole with a trowel just large enough to hold a clean tin can.

2 Put the can in the hole so that the rim is just below the soil surface.

3 Push four pebbles into the soil around the submerged can.

4 Place a flat tile over the trap. Camouflage with twigs.

MAKING A SLUG OR SNAIL TRAP

Slugs and snails can munch through your plants, so trap them and release away from your garden.

1 Eat half a grapefruit. Turn the skin upside down and place on the ground by target plants.

2 Leave the trap overnight, then next morning see who's taken the bait!

MAKING AN EARWIG TRAP

If you see earwigs on your crysanthemums, dahlias or artichokes, trap them and put on the compost heap.

1 Fill a clay pot with hay or straw. Push a stout cane (stake) into the ground between plants.

2 Upturn the pot and balance it on the end of the cane. Earwigs will be drawn to the pot.

Controlling the bad guys

Most of the time you can ignore the following creatures, but occasionally they cause problems in particular areas of the garden, such as the vegetable plot. Picking the culprits off by hand is a quick and environmentally friendly way of tackling many garden pests, but you may need to take more action. Here are some of the common culprits:

Aphids Also known as greenfly, aphids can be white, pink or black. These tiny sap-sucking insects attack shoot tips and flower-buds, causing leaves and blooms to shrivel. They also spread viruses. Rub off colonies between your thumb and index finger or blast them off plants with a jet of water from a hosepipe (garden hose). Encourage natural predators, such as lacewings, ladybirds (ladybugs) and insect-eating birds.

Caterpillars Many caterpillers grow into beautiful butterflies and moths, but some species have huge appetites for certain plants, such as cabbages and other brassicas. You'll need keen eyesight as they can be well camouflaged. Pick off even the tiny ones as soon as you spot them and move to a wild patch, long grass or hedge. Stop adult butterflies laying eggs on crops by covering plants with a fine garden mesh or horticultural fleece (floating row covers).
CAUTION Some caterpillars have poisonous or irritant hairs or bristles. Don't touch them if you aren't sure, or you can wear gloves.

Earwigs These minibeasts are not usually a problem in the garden, despite their fearsome-looking pincers. However, if you grow globe artichokes, dahlias or chrysanthemums, they can hide in the flowers and munch away unnoticed. Trap (*see box above*) and transfer to the compost heap.

Slugs and snails These molluscs love to eat big ragged holes in delicate flowers, young leaves and seedlings. They hide away during the daytime, so the best way to catch them in the act is to wait until nightfall. Ask your parents to go on a hunt with you after dark with a torch (flashlight). Wear thin gloves if you don't like the slime! You could also put out grapefruit traps (*see box above*). Take collected molluscs to a wild patch well away from vulnerable plants. You can also try barriers of grit (which they don't like to crawl over) around targeted plants or position copper tape around pot rims.

▲ *Blast off aphids with a strong jet of water.*

▲ *Wearing gloves, hand-pick and relocate caterpillars.*

Hands-on basics

In the following pages you will discover many of the skills you need as a gardener, from making compost out of recycled materials to collecting and saving water, pruning, weeding and deadheading. Soon you will be growing your own plants from seed (collected from your own garden) and learning how to take different kinds of cuttings.

Clever compost

Compost is made up of rotted down scraps, prunings, grass cuttings and cardboard. Not only will your garden benefit from the rich mix of plant foods and other helpful ingredients, but you'll also be able to do more recycling and throw away a lot less, which is good for the environment. This handy compost technique is easy to carry out in a spare corner of the garden, provided you follow a few simple rules.

you will need

- **border fork**
- **stiff plastic clematis mesh**, 1m/3ft width
- **1.2m/4ft bamboo canes (stakes)**, 4–5
- **rubber mallet**
- **Cane Heads** (see page 125)
- **garden twine** or **plastic-coated wire plant ties**
- **plastic refuse sack (garbage bag)**
- **clothes pegs (clothspins)**
- **scissors**
- **non-woody prunings**
- **annual weeds**, seed-heads removed
- **secateurs (pruners)**
- **kitchen waste**, such as raw fruit and vegetable
- **teabags**
- **coffee grounds** and **paper filters**
- **cardboard**, ripped up into small pieces
- **cardboard kitchen roll inners**
- **compostable food packaging**
- **fibre** or **recycled pulp egg boxes** or **cartons**
- **grass cuttings**

plastic refuse sack

fibre egg box

banana skins

1 Fork over the ground to loosen the soil and improve drainage. Arrange the plastic clematis mesh to form a circle, and knock in bamboo canes with a mallet to keep the mesh upright. Adult supervision is required.

2 To protect your eyes while you work, push on cane (stake) tops. Tie the mesh securely to the canes at several points along their length using garden twine or plastic-coated wire plant ties.

3 Line the mesh with a refuse sack, attaching it with pegs. Make a few holes in the bottom of the sack with scissors and ensure that it is touching the ground to allow worms to enter.

4 Put some non-woody prunings and annual weeds in the bottom to provide drainage. Ask an adult to help you cut them up with secateurs if they are too hard to break up by hand.

5 Over a period of several weeks, continue adding alternating layers of wetter and drier materials to the refuse sack. For example, follow wet or damp material, such as vegetable scraps, teabags and coffee grounds or used filters from the kitchen, with dry material, such as torn-up cardboard, egg boxes and compostable food packaging, then add grass cuttings on top.

6 When the bag is full, but not too heavy, unclip the pegs and lift it out of the mesh surround. It's easier to do this with two people. Tie off the top of the bag with garden twine.

 = Watch out! Sharp or dangerous tool in use. = Watch out! Adult help is needed.

7 Position a new plastic sack in the mesh and begin filling it with garden and kitchen waste as described. Meanwhile, put the filled, sealed bags in a shady corner of the garden, standing on bare earth.

8 After a year or more, the contents of the bags will have turned into compost. Coarse, twiggy material will take longer to break down. Dig the compost into borders to improve your soil.

TOP TIPS

▶ Mix kitchen scraps or lawn clippings with absorbent materials, such as shredded cardboard and egg cartons, to avoid the compost becoming too wet and airless, which would make it slimy.
▶ Water the contents of the bag occasionally during hot weather if necessary.

Be water wise!

During hot weather there is less rain and plants get thirsty more quickly, so you need to give them a drink more often. It is important, though, that we all try and save water in the house and the garden, especially in the summer. So, here are some simple ideas for collecting and reusing water for the garden, as well as ways to help plants stay moist for longer.

you will need

- **watering can**
- **spade**
- **chipped bark, garden compost, manure, coir** or **cocoa shells,** for mulching
- **plastic bag** or **sheet**
- **scissors**
- **crocks (clay pieces)**
- **gravel**
- **moisture-retentive potting compost (soil mix)** with **added water-retaining gel crystals**
- **plant**
- **bucket of water**
- **glass** or **acrylic chippings**

bark

cocoa shells

1 Mulching is an excellent way of sealing moisture into the ground around plant roots but it needs to be at least 8cm/3in deep to work, and the ground must be damp beforehand. Check the area and water if necessary.

2 Apply mulch from early to late spring when the ground is naturally moist. Shovel on bark, garden compost, manure, coir or cocoa shells. Keep it clear of the neck of plants. Adult supervision is required.

3 Plants in porous clay or terracotta pots lose moisture more quickly than those in wood, glazed ceramic or plastic pots. Lining clay pots with thin plastic before planting them reduces moisture-loss.

4 You can recycle thin plastic bags. To avoid drainage problems, pull the bag through the hole at the bottom of the pot and cut the end off with scissors. Adult supervision is required.

5 Add crocks and gravel for drainage, then pour in some moisture-retentive compost with added water-retaining gel crystals. Some mixtures have this in already. Try the plant for size.

6 Plunge a plant in a bucket of water and wait for the bubbles to stop. Plant, adding compost, leaving a gap at the top. Trim the plastic to be level with the top of the pot.

TOP TIPS

▶ Create a shallow, circular groove around newly planted specimens and bank the soil up to stop water from the can running away. It then pools and sinks in around the roots right where it's needed.

▶ Another trick is to cut the bottom out of a large plastic bottle and bury it, top end down, next to the plant. Water into the bottle to reach the roots directly.

 = Watch out! Sharp or dangerous tool in use.   = Watch out! Adult help is needed.

7 Mulches can also be decorative and made from materials that don't rot down, such as glass or acrylic chips. They can still help to conserve moisture. Water the newly positioned plant thoroughly.

8 Water in the kitchen used for peeling and preparing fruit and vegetables might contain soil or dirt but it's perfectly fine for watering plants. Instead of pouring it down the sink, hold the peelings back with your hand, pour the water on the garden, then compost the peelings.

TOP TIP

► Water in the cool of morning or evening, not in the heat of the day. Concentrate on new plantings and give vulnerable plants a good long drink at ground level under their leaves rather than lots of little overhead sprinklings.

Rainwater collector

Collecting rainwater in a special butt (barrel) is good for the environment and many plants prefer it to tap water.

you will need

- **water butt (barrel) connection kit**
- **hacksaw** (for adult use only)
- **water butt**
- **water butt extension kit** (optional)
- **water butt stand** or **bricks**
- **childproof lid**
- **watering can**

watering can

TOP TIP

▶ Rainwater is perfect for most houseplants, especially if the tap water is hard. Some plants dislike the shock of cold water so fill indoor watering cans with water from the butt and let it warm up.

1 You can fit a water butt to a drainpipe (downspout) on the house or garage and, if you fit guttering and drainpipes to greenhouses and shed , you can collect rainwater from them too if you have another butt.

2 Ask an adult to help you set up one or more water butts in your selected position. Buy a connection kit that diverts water from a drainpipe to the butt, but which prevents the water butt from overflowing.

3 Ask an adult to cut the drainpipe with a hacksaw so that you can fit the water diverter, following packet instructions. Push the flexible pipe into the top of the butt. A water butt stand or bricks raises the butt to allow for watering cans.

4 When it rains, average-size water butts quickly fill up, but they also empty quickly too! Make the most of the work you've already done, if you like, by connecting another butt using an extension kit, which collects any overflow.

5 To prevent accidents and to stop debris falling into the water, it is essential that you fit a childproof lid on to the butt. Keeping out sunlight also stops green algae forming. Use a space-saving butt for tight corners.

 = Watch out! Sharp or dangerous tool in use.   = Watch out! Adult help is needed.

Mini cloches and slug guards

Don't throw away plastic bottles. You can use them to make a mini cloche (hot cap), a slug barrier or a mini propagator.

you will need
- **large, clear plastic bottles**
- **scissors**

TOP TIP

▶ It is easy to make a mini propagator at home from plastic bottles. Ask an adult to help you cut the middle section out of a bottle so that the top and bottom segments fit neatly together. Make some holes in the base for drainage and you have a propagator.

Step 1

Step 2

1 Ask an adult to help you cut the bottom off the plastic bottle using a pair of scissors. Cut as near to the bottom as you can so you have more bottle to work with. Cut off the top to make a mini cloche. Save the middle section.

2 Protect seedlings and young plantlets by covering them with the bottle cloche. Push it into the ground to stop it blowing over. The plastic keeps the plant warm and helps to protect it from slug attack.

3 The middle part of the bottle can be used to make a barrier for seedlings against slugs, especially in the vegetable patch where there are lots of tasty temptations! Simply push the base into the soil so it doesn't blow over.

4 If you leave the lid screwed on the bottle cloche, the air inside will become warm and moist, which is ideal for plant growth. As the plantlet gets stronger you can remove the lid to increase the airflow and finally remove the cloche altogether.

plastic bottle

Plant makeovers!

Two jobs that really tidy up the garden are weeding and deadheading. When you remove faded blooms you also encourage more to follow, especially with annuals, which can stop flowering if they are allowed to create seeds. Pruning also allows you to control a plant's shape and size and to remove damaged, diseased or weak growth. Note, not all plants require pruning and you should only use secateurs with an adult's help and supervision.

you will need
- **flower scissors**
- **secateurs** or **hand pruners**
- **gardening gloves (optional)**
- **hand shears**
- **hand** or **border fork**
- **bark chips**, **pine needles**, **coir** or **cocoa shells**

TOP TIP
▶ Prune deciduous shrubs and climbers (those that lose their leaves in winter) according to when they flower. For spring- and early summer-flowering kinds, such as forsythia, mock orange, weigela and large-flowering clematis, prune immediately after flowering. For late summer- and autumn-flowering kinds, such as *Clematis viticella* varieties, butterfly bush, and patio and bush roses, prune in spring.

1 Most single, wiry-stemmed flowers are easier to deadhead with flower scissors. Cut the faded bloom off at the base of the stem rather than just behind the head. Adult supervision is required.

2 Some soft or fleshy-stemmed flowers, such as those on this day lily, can be pinched out with your thumb and index finger, leaving the freshly opened blooms and buds in the head to develop further.

3 With flower spires, cut the whole stem off at the base, rather than picking off individual blooms. Do this with plants such as hosta (shown here), penstemon, campanula and hollyhock.

4 Deadhead flowering shrubs, like roses, with secateurs or hand pruners. Ask an adult for help, and wear gloves if necessary. Cut away dead, diseased or weak growth at the same time.

5 Trimming with hand shears removes faded flowers on plants such as lavender and marguerite daisy and means you can shape the plant. Adult supervision is required.

6 Annual weeds are usually easy to pull out by hand, especially when still young and with a small root system. Add to the compost heap, having first removed any seed-heads.

7 Perennial weeds living one year to the next usually have a big, tough taproot or creeping root network. Dig out as much of the root as you can with a hand or border fork because remaining pieces make more weeds.

8 Mulch the area with a thick bark, pine needle, coir or cocoa shell mulch (at least 8cm/3in deep) to prevent more weeds coming up in the flower border. Weeds compete with flowers for food, water and light, so need to be controlled.

cocoa shells

secateurs

bucket of weeding tools

Seed harvest

Collecting your own seed is satisfying and so easy! Fresh seed germinates more quickly than old stored seed, and harvesting flower and even vegetable seed from the garden saves money too. The main thing to bear in mind is to keep everything dry when harvesting, processing or cleaning and storing the seed. Don't gather seed from dead or diseased plants. Seal envelopes in an airtight container and keep in a cool place for up to two years.

you will need
- **scissors**
- **sheet** of **paper**
- **white envelopes**
- **coloured pens, pencils** or **crayons**
- **paper bag**

coloured pencils

plant list
* **Annual poppy**
  Papaver spp.
* **Bellflower**
  Campanula persicifolia
* **Big quaking grass**
  Briza maxima
* **Cosmos, Mexican aster**
  Cosmos bipinnatus
* **Dusty miller, rose campion**
  Lychnis coronaria
* **English lavender**
  Lavandula angustifolia
* **Everlasting sweet pea**
  Lathyrus latifolius
* **French and African marigold**
  Tagetes

* **Granny's bonnet, columbine**
  Aquilegia vulgaris
* **Love-in-a-mist**
  Nigella damascena
* **Pot marigold**
  Calendula officinalis
* **Purple top verbena**
  Verbena bonariensis
* **Sunflower**
  Helianthus annuus

sunflower seeds

1 When a flower-head has faded, dried off and produced seed, as shown here with this lavender, cut the stems using scissors and take them inside. Gather one species at a time. Adult supervision is required.

2 Some seed drops easily when it is ripe, but for others you will need to keep the mature flower-heads for about a week in a warm, dry place. When you are ready to collect, fold a piece of paper in half.

3 Holding the lavender heads over the paper, gently rub the old flowers between your fingers to release the shiny black seeds. Use the same method for purple top verbena.

4 Carefully lift the two halves of the paper to form a scoop so that you can direct the seed into an envelope. Write the plant name and date on the envelope, then seal.

5 Hand-decorated packets of seed make lovely presents. Use pens or crayons to draw pictures of the plant in flower on the envelope so you know at a glance what it is.

6 For seed that scatters easily, such as quaking grass, dusty miller, poppy and bellflower, put a paper bag over the heads, cut the stems and, holding the bag securely, tip upside-down.

     = Watch out! Sharp or dangerous tool in use.   = Watch out! Adult help is needed.

7 After a week in a warm place, much of this *Aquilegia* seed will have dropped into the bag. Empty the seed on to a sheet of paper. Hold the pods upside down and tap to shake out the remainder.

8 Try to separate as much debris or chaff (remains of the pod or flower) from the seed as possible. With lightweight debris and larger, heavier seed, gently blow the chaff away.

FACT FILE

SEEDS OF CHANGE

Not all plants sown from collected seed will end up looking the same as the original plant you collected it from.

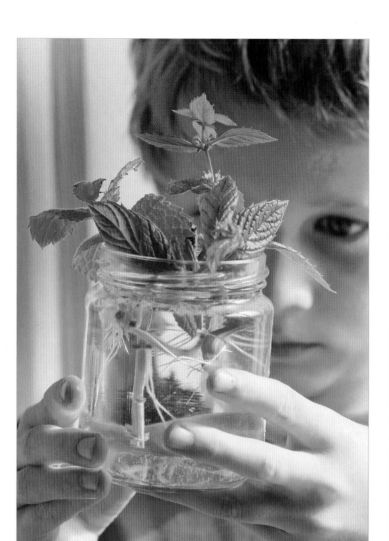

Glass jar cuttings

It's fun to try rooting all kinds of cuttings in water, including houseplants, patio plants, herbs and shrubs. Some, such as African violets, root from a single leaf!

you will need
- scissors
- clean glass jars
- small pots
- potting compost (soil mix)
- **kitchen foil** or **waxed paper** (optional)
- **elastic (rubber) band** (optional)

plant list
- ✳ **African violet**
  Saintpaulia ionantha
- ✳ **Busy Lizzie**
  Impatiens spp. and varieties
- ✳ **Coleus**
  Solenostemon scutellarioides
- ✳ **Geranium**
  Pelargonium spp.
- ✳ **Giant inch plant ,spiderwort**
  Tradescantia fluminensis
- ✳ **Mint**
  Mentha spp.

busy Lizzie

1 Cut off healthy young shoots with scissors (adult supervision is required) or break off with your hands. Have a jar of water ready.

2 Prepare the cuttings, in this case mint, by nipping off the lower leaves. You just need a few at the top of the cutting. Trim just below the bottom leaf joint.

3 Put a handful of cuttings into the glass jar so that the stems are covered with water. Place on a warm, light window ledge.

4 After a while you will see tiny roots starting to appear from the leaf joints along the submerged stems. Allow these to grow a little more.

5 When a good root system has developed, pot the cuttings up.

6 Plants with hairy or felted leaves, such as African violet, or ones that dislike wet conditions, such as geraniums, must be rooted with their leaves held above the surface of the water.

7 Fit a piece of foil or waxed paper over a glass jar and hold it in place with an elastic band.

8 Make holes in the foil or paper with scissors (adult supervision is required). Slot the cuttings or African violet leaves through the holes and pour enough water to cover the base of the stems through one of the holes.

African violet

 = Watch out! Sharp or dangerous tool in use. = Watch out! Adult help is needed.

Baby plants

It's possible to make more plants from semi-ripe cuttings in summer. You'll be amazed at how many plants you can raise from just one little piece!

you will need

- knife
- chopping board
- **small pots** or a **plastic bottle**, cut in half
- **cuttings compost (soil mix)**
- pencil
- plant labels
- pen
- **bowl** of water
- plastic bag
- elastic (rubber) band
- slender garden canes (stakes), 3–4
- **medium pots**, filled with cuttings compost
- scissors

plant list

- ❋ **Beard tongue**
  Penstemon cvs.
- ❋ **Butterfly bush**
  Buddleja davidii
- ❋ **Geranium**
  Pelargonium
- ❋ **Hydrangea (mop head and lacecap)**
  Hydrangea macrophylla cvs.
- ❋ **Lavender**
  Lavandula spp. and cvs.
- ❋ **Sage**
  Salvia officinalis and cvs.
- ❋ **Thyme**
  Thymus spp.

1 In late summer you can take semi-ripe or heel cuttings from plants such as sage, shown here. Pull off side shoots with a piece of the main stem (heel) attached.

2 Trim off lower leaves with a knife on a chopping board. Ask an adult to help you. Trim away any long strips of bark.

3 Put some grit in the bottom of the pots or bottle. Make planting holes with a pencil. Put a cutting in each and firm in. Label.

4 Water the compost. Fit a clear plastic bag over the pot, support with canes and hold in place with an elastic band, or fit the top of the bottle over the bottom.

5 Place the pot or bottle in a light position, such as a windowsill, and leave for 2–8 weeks to root. When the plants have grown about 2cm/¾in they can be very carefully transplanted into slightly bigger individual pots. Take care not to damage the fragile roots when you move the plants.

6 Softwood or tip cuttings of plants such as courgette (zucchini), tomato and fuchsia are taken earlier in the year using the top of a non-flowering shoot. Pinch off a cutting (see Step 1), trim the base under a leaf joint (as shown) with scissors (adult supervision is required), take off lower leaves and pot up in the same way.

Dividing plants

When planning a new border it can be costly to buy all the plants you need to fill the space. Dividing newly purchased plants or digging up and dividing perennials already in the garden can be a great solution. Adult supervision is required for cutting the root-ball.

you will need

- **slightly potbound plant** with **lots of young shoots** (*see* Plant List), 1
- **bucket** of **water**
- **old kitchen knife**
- **chopping board**
- **15–20cm/6–8in plastic plant pots**, 5
- **peat-free potting compost (soil mix)**
- **slow-release fertilizer granules**
- **watering can**
- **plant labels**, 5
- **pencil**

plant list

- ✳ **Aster**
  Aster
- ✳ **Bee balm**
  Monarda
- ✳ **Bellflower**
  Campanula
- ✳ **Black-eyed Susan**
  Rudbeckia
- ✳ **Border phlox**
  Phlox
- ✳ **Crane's bill**
  Geranium
- ✳ **Day lily**
  Hemerocallis
- ✳ **Funkia, plantain lily**
  Hosta
- ✳ **Ice plant, showy stonecrop**
  Sedum spectabile
- ✳ **Michaelmas daisy**
  Aster
- ✳ **Ornamental sage**
  Salvia
- ✳ **Peruvian lily**
  Alstroemeria
- ✳ **Purple coneflower**
  Echinacea
- ✳ **Shasta daisy**
  Leucanthemum x *superbum*
- ✳ **Sneezeweed**
  Helenium
- ✳ **Turtle's head**
  Chelone
- ✳ **Yarrow, milfoil**
  Achillea

purple coneflower

day lily

1 In spring, look for potted plants that are sprouting lots of new shoots, either in the garden or at a garden centre. When you gently ease the root-ball out of its pot you should see strong root growth.

2 It doesn't matter if it is slightly potbound – you will be giving room to grow when you divide it. Plunge the plant in a bucket of water and wait for the bubbles to stop. Try pulling the roots apart with your hands.

3 Sometimes it is easier to cut the root-ball with an old kitchen knife rather than pulling it. It doesn't need to be very sharp but take care when cutting and ask an adult to help.

4 Depending on the size of the plant and how many pieces of shoot (each with a reasonable-size chunk of root) you can separate off, you could end up with 3–7 divisions.

5 Plant or pot each small division into a plastic plant pot three-quarters filled with potting compost mixed with some slow-release fertilizer. Follow the packet instructions.

6 The pot should be large enough to give the plant plenty of room to grow, but not too huge. Firm the soil around the roots with your hands, water and label.

7 Stand the young plants in a sheltered spot to grow on. Don't allow the compost to dry out. When the pots are filled with roots, and the shoots are growing strongly, plant out in the garden.

TOP TIP

▶ Divide herbaceous perennial plants every 2–3 years in spring or autumn. Ask an adult to help you dig the plant out, and, using two garden forks back to back as levers, prise (pry) the roots apart. Chop out dead areas. Replant the younger sections in improved soil.

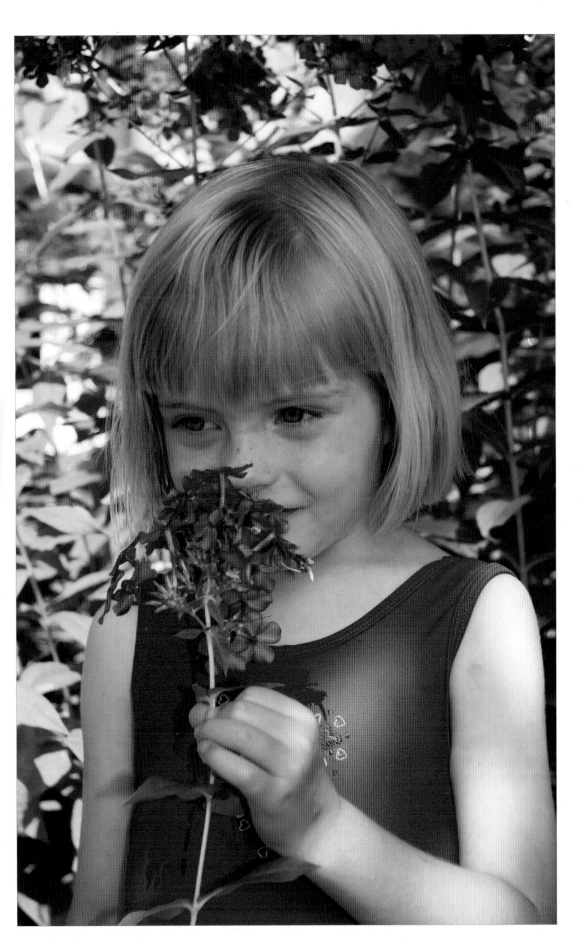

Hardwood cuttings

Though slow, this is one of the easiest ways to propagate shrubs and roses as well as several kinds of fruit.

you will need
- trowel
- digging spade
  (optional)
- washed horticultural sand
- secateurs (pruners)
- watering can

plant list

- ✳ **Blackcurrant**
  Ribes nigrum
- ✳ **Butterfly bush**
  Buddleja davidii
- ✳ **Bush, patio and shrub roses**
  Rosa
- ✳ **Coloured-stemmed dogwoods**
  Cornus spp.
- ✳ **Common aspen**
  Populus tremula
- ✳ **Forsythia**
  Forsythia
- ✳ **Gooseberry**
  Ribes uva-crispa
- ✳ **Mock orange**
  Philadelphus
- ✳ **Ornamental elder**
  Sambucus
- ✳ **Privet**
  Ligustrum
- ✳ **Shrubby (box) honeysuckle**
  Lonicera nitida
- ✳ **Weigela**
  Weigela cvs.
- ✳ **Willow**
  Salix

rose

privet

1 Prepare a narrow trench in a sheltered part of a border where you won't need to dig for a year. Use a trowel or ask an adult to help you open up a slit in the ground with a digging spade. The trench or slit should be about 5cm/2in wide and 20cm/8in deep when you have finished. Reserve the soil.

2 To help the cuttings roots and to improve poor drainage, add some sand to the trench.

3 With adult help, take some hardwood cuttings from one of the plants in the Plant List. Cut stems about the thickness of a pencil and 15–30cm/ 6–12in long with secateurs.

4 To help you remember which way up the cuttings grow, cut the top off at an angle. Cut off any soft shoot tips.

5 Put the cuttings upright into the trench so that about two-thirds of the stem is below ground. The angled cut should be at the top!

6 Move the soil back into the trench and firm the cuttings in well with your hands. Water as necessary during dry spells.

7 When you gently lift the cuttings the following autumn, they will have roots and new shoots and be ready for planting directly into a border.

(!) = Watch out! Sharp or dangerous tool in use. = Watch out! Adult help is needed.

Rooting runners

This propagation method takes advantage of the way some plants grow, sending out stems with baby plants on the end that are ready to root.

you will need
- **plants** with **offshoots/runners** (see Plant List)
- **plastic pots**
- **cuttings compost (soil mix)**, such as John Innes No.1 or other mix
- **trowel**
- **plastic-coated training wire**, cut into short lengths

plant list
- ✳ **Bugle**
  Ajuga reptans
- ✳ **Ivy**
  Hedera helix
- ✳ **Lesser periwinkle**
  Vinca minor
- ✳ **Pick-a-back plant, youth on age**
  Tolmiea menziesii
- ✳ **Spider plant**
  Chlorophytum comosum
- ✳ **Strawberry**
  Fragaria

spider plant

1 Some houseplants, including the familiar spider plant and pick-a-back plant, are fun and easy to root from runners. Fill a pot with compost using a trowel.

2 Pin the individual babies with lengths of wire bent over so that the base of each is in contact with the soil.

3 In summer, strawberry plants make lots of runners and you can increase your strawberry bed very quickly and easily by rooting the babies. Either pin down the runners in contact with soil using wire pins (as in Step 2) in the border or bury a pot of cuttings compost next to the plant and pin into that.

4 Once the babies have made their own roots you can cut the stem attaching them to the mother plant and pot up the plantlets individually.

5 Many plants, such as ivy and periwinkle, root where they touch the ground at each leaf cluster. Pin down shoots to speed rooting.

TOP TIP
▶ You can get many shrubs (such as cotoneaster), climbers, (such as honeysuckle), and fruits (such as blackberry) to root, by bending a stem to lie on, or loop down into, the ground and out again. Hold in place with a stone so that the stem is in contact with soil. This is called layering.

Growing things to eat

You'll be amazed at how many different kinds of tasty herbs, sweet and juicy fruits and fresh vegetables you can grow even if you don't have any beds or borders. Lots of crops can be raised in pots, troughs and hanging baskets. This chapter is all about using your garden fork to make food for your table fork!

A basketful of squash

Courgettes or zucchini (that's their Italian name) are rewarding types of squash that start to crop early and keep producing until autumn. Grow in large containers, such as this log basket, or in well-manured ground, from seed or bought plants. You'll only need one or two. Try a round, striped or coloured variety for something different. Crop when fruits are small and tender. If you leave them for too long then courgettes turn into marrows! Wear gloves if your skin is sensitive to the bristles.

you will need

- **courgette (zucchini) seeds** (*see* Plant List), 1–3
- **small plant pots**, 1–3
- **peat-free seed** and **cuttings compost (soil mix)**
- **windowsill propagator**
- **wicker log basket**
- **heavy-duty trash liner**
- **scissors**
- **gravel**
- **trowel**
- **peat-free potting compost** with **added loam (soil mix)**, 1 x 80-litre/21-gallon bag
- **watering can**
- **liquid plant food**, for edible plants

plant list

✳ **Green types of courgette (*Cucurbita pepo*):**
'Bambino' F1 (patio type)
'Black Forest' F1 (climber)
'Defender' F1 (virus-resistant)
'Jaguar' (no bristles)
'Tosca' (compact, mildew resistant)
'Tristan' F1 (no bristles)
'Venus' F1 (compact)

✳ **Yellow types of *Cucurbita pepo*:**
'Gold Rush' F1
'Jemmer' F1 (round fruits)
'Parador' F1
'Soleil' F1

courgette plant

1 Sow the seeds 1cm/½in deep in mid-spring in pots of seed and cuttings compost. Stand in a propagator on a warm windowsill. After the seeds have germinated, remove the seedlings from the propagator.

2 When the young plants are growing well, begin to harden them off using a lightly shaded cold frame or by standing the plants out during the day for increasing amounts of time (*see* page 13).

3 After 10–15 days the seedlings can be planted outside. Line a log basket with a bin liner. Make holes in the bottom with scissors and add a layer of gravel using a trowel.

4 Cut open one end of a large bag of peat-free potting compost and turn it upside down into the basket. This is a two-person job so ask an adult to help. Shake out the contents.

5 Break up any lumps in the compost with your hands. Water the compost with a watering can if it is dry. The top layer should be thoroughly moist and ready for planting.

6 Plant one or two courgette plants in the compost, depending on the variety. Some patio varieties, such as 'Bambino' are dwarf and compact, so you could fit two in.

7 Water in the courgettes and keep them well watered as they are thirsty plants. Feed with a liquid fertlizer, such as tomato food, every 14 days. Avoid overhead watering, which promotes powdery mildew.

FACT FILE

ALL SHAPES, SIZES AND SHADES

Courgettes come in a surprising range of types. There are green- or yellow-skinned varieties, ones with striped skins, and as well as the usual cylindrical courgettes, you can grow ones with fruits shaped like tennis balls!

yellow courgettes

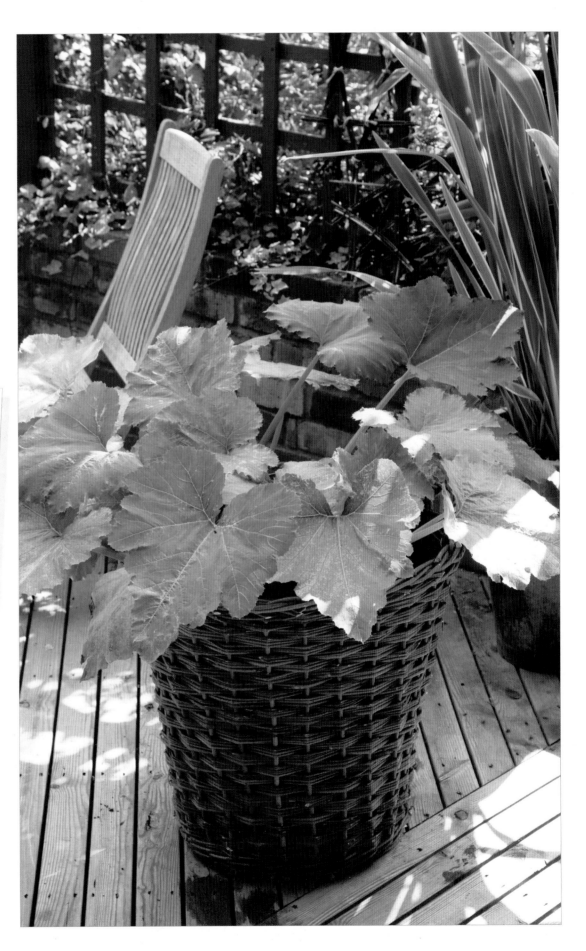

a basketful of squash **53**

Grow bag garden

Even if you don't have any beds or borders you can still grow many vegetables and herbs in bags. For this project, you'll need a sunny wall. Although you could grow your own plants from seed in early spring, it is much easier to buy plants.

you will need
- **range** of **edible plants**, (see Plant List)
- **felt-tipped pen**
- **grow bags (soil mix bags)**, 3
- **scissors**
- **bucket** of **water**
- **bamboo canes (stakes)**, 9
- **corks** or **cane protectors**, 9
- **garden twine**
- **watering can**
- **liquid plant food**, for edible plants

plant list
- ✳ **3 cherry tomato plants**
  Lycopersicon esculentum 'Gardener's Delight' or 'Super Sweet 100'
- ✳ **3 aubergine (eggpant) plants (patio variety)**
  Solanum melongena 'Baby Belle', 'Bonica', 'Baby Rosanna' or 'Mohican'
- ✳ **3 basil plants**
  Ocimum basilicum 'Genovese'
- ✳ **3 bell pepper plants (patio variety)**
  Capsicum annuum var. *annuum* (Grossum Group) 'Redskin' or 'Mohawk'
- ✳ **1 tray of French marigolds**
  Tagetes patula

TOP TIP
▶ The compost (soil) in the bags is usually compacted. Ask an adult to help you shake the bags and fluff up the compost to make it easier for the plants to root into it.

1 Using one of the larger plants as a template, centre it on a grow bag and draw around the base of the pot with a felt-tipped pen. Repeat to make three evenly spaced circles down the middle of each grow bag.

2 With adult supervision, cut out the circles with a pair of scissors. Prepare a planting hole with your hands. Soak the plants by plunging in a bucket of water until the bubbles stop.

3 Plant the tomatoes in one of the grow bags and lightly firm with your fingers. Tomatoes can be prone to whitefly and traditionally marigolds are used to repel these pests.

TOP TIP
▶ Plants that have already been hardened off are widely available from most garden centres in early summer. If you buy them from a protected glasshouse area, however, you'll need to do the hardening off yourself (see page 13). It takes about two to three weeks. Don't plant outside until after the risk of late frosts has passed.

4 Make a series of small holes along the front of the grow bag with scissors or simply snip 'X' shapes and peel back the plastic. Plant French marigolds in the holes.

5 Plant the aubergines in a different grow bag and lightly firm with your fingers. If you need to make the holes slightly bigger, snip the circle in four places to ease the root-ball in.

6 Like the pungent French marigolds, aromatic basil is another 'companion plant', helping to naturally protect plants from pests. Plant the basil in holes around the edge of one of the grow bags.

7 Plant the peppers in the final grow bag. Insert tall canes propped against the wall for the tomatoes and stick short canes into the compost for the other plants. Top with corks.

8 Loosely tie in the plants to the canes with garden twine as they grow. Water the grow bags daily. Once flowers appear, feed the plants regularly with liquid plant food, following instructions on the bottle.

twine and scissors

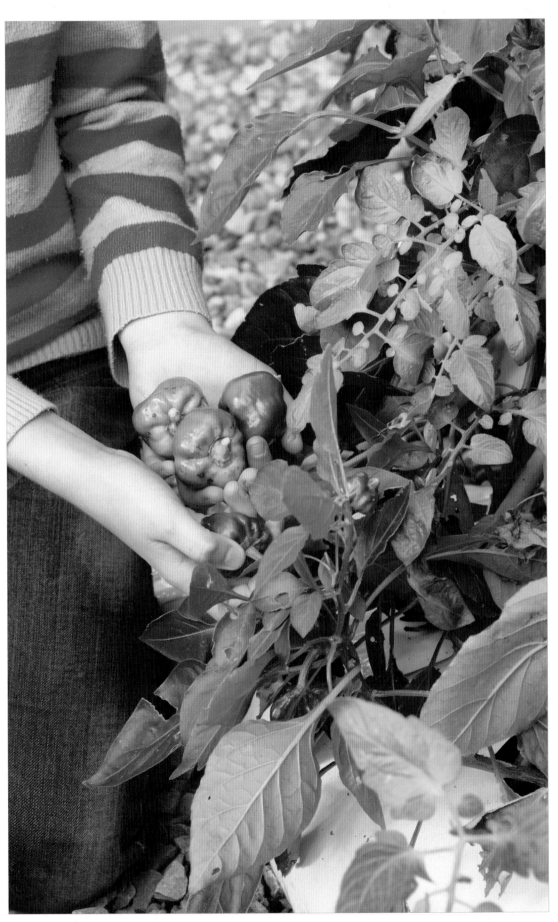

Patio veggie garden

Quick-growing summer vegetables can be grown in all kinds of containers on the patio. For instance, early potatoes are easy to grow in plastic crates (with drainage holes punched through the base). It feels great to be able to pick and eat fresh produce grown just by the back door and there are so many things to try. As well as growing from seed, you can buy potted seedlings.

you will need
- **assorted pots** and **containers**
- **utility knife** (for adult use only)
- **crocks** (clay pieces) and **gravel**
- **peat-free potting compost** with **added loam** (soil mix)
- **slow-release fertilizer granules**
- **bamboo canes** (stakes)
- **wire**
- **garden twine**
- **watering can**
- **liquid plant food**, for edible plants

FACT FILE
SMALL IS BEAUTIFUL
Look out for special dwarf or patio varieties designed for growing in pots. Also use quick-to-mature salads and vegetables that can be picked when still young and tender, such as baby carrots and beetroot (beet). The tomato variety 'Totem' with medium-size fruits and aubergine (eggplant) 'Baby Rosanna' crop in 20–25cm/ 8–10in pots, so are ideal for a small space.

tomato 'Totem'

plant list
- ✳ **Baby beetroot (beet)**
  Beta vulgaris 'Boltardy'
- ✳ **Dwarf green bean**
  Phaseolus vulgaris var. *nanus* 'Maxi'
- ✳ **Dwarf runner bean**
  Phaseolus coccineus 'Hestia'
- ✳ **Lettuce**
  Lactuca sativa 'Red Salad Bowl'
- ✳ **Patio courgette (zucchini)**
  Cucurbita pepo 'Bambino' F1
- ✳ **Radicchio/Italian chicory**
  Cichorium intybus var. *sativum*
- ✳ **Radish**
  Raphanus sativus 'Cherry Belle'
- ✳ **Round carrot**
  Daucus carota 'Parmex'
- ✳ **Salad onion (scallion)**
  Allium cepa 'White Lisbon'

1 Any containers you use, whether plant pots and troughs or recycled containers, need to have good drainage. Ask an adult to make holes. Cover these with crocks and gravel.

2 Fill the containers with peat-free compost mixed with some slow-release fertilizer granules. Take a strip of radicchio plantlets, pull the roots apart and plant, firming in gently.

3 For other mild-tasting salad leaves, sow lettuce, such as 'Red Salad Bowl', a wavy edged oak leaf type (shown here). The small, hearting lettuce 'Little Gem' is also a good choice.

4 Some vegetables are quick to grow from seed and you can get several crops in one year. Sow radishes, salad leaves, round carrots and salad onions every two weeks.

5 Raise or buy baby courgette plants of 'Bambino' and plant three in a large tub. Give them a warm, sheltered place to begin with and ensure the plants are hardened off.

6 Plant dwarf patio varieties of runner and French beans. These will need support, so make a wigwam of canes, coil round some wire and tie in the stems with garden twine.

7 Water all the seedlings. Leafy vegetables and plants with developing fruits need regular watering. Group the containers together to make watering easier.

8 There's only a small amount of compost in each container, so use a slow-release fertilizer at planting time and supplement with regular liquid plant food.

Colourful veg

Some vegetables are too attractive to be kept hidden away in the vegetable plot. Runner beans (main picture) make beautiful flowering climbers and some squash and pumpkin plants can be trained over trellises and archways. Red- or purple-leaved lettuce, curly kale, beetroot and ruby Swiss chard add colour to containers. Try mixing in some edible blooms, pots of purple-podded French beans and tomato-filled baskets.

you will need

- **small pots** and **seed trays**
- **peat-free seed** and **cuttings compost** (soil mix)
- **assorted plants** (*see* Plant List)
- **containers, window boxes** and **hanging baskets**
- **loam-based potting compost** (soil mix)
- **twiggy sticks**
- **sharp knife**
- **barrel**

plant list

- ✳ **Aubergine (eggplant)**
  Solanum melongena 'Baby Rosanna'; 'Bonica'; 'Mohican'
- ✳ **Beetroot (beet)**
  Beta vulgaris 'Bull's Blood'
- ✳ **Courgette, yellow (zucchini)**
  Cucurbita pepo 'One Ball', 'Gold Rush' F1
- ✳ **Curly kale (borecole)**
  Brassica oleracea 'Redbor' F1
- ✳ **Dwarf bush tomatoes**
  Lycopersicon esculentum 'Tumbler' F1, 'Totem'
- ✳ **Dwarf French (green) bean**
  Phaseolus vulgaris 'Purple Queen', 'Purple Teepee'

- ✳ **Pumpkin**
  Cucurbita pepo 'Baby Bear', 'Jack Be Little'
- ✳ **Radicchio/Italian chicory**
  Cichorium intybus var. *sativum*
- ✳ **Red cabbage**
  Brassica oleracea var. *capitata* 'Red Jewel'
- ✳ **Red lettuce**
  Lactuca sativa 'Delicato', 'Red Salad Bowl'
- ✳ **Runner bean**
  Phaseolus coccineus
- ✳ **Squash, patty pan type**
  Cucurbita pepo 'Sunburst' F1
- ✳ **Swiss chard**
  Beta vulgaris var. *flavescens* subsp. *cicla* 'Bright Lights'

1 Fill small pots and seed trays with compost and plant whichever seeds you like. Curly kale is good for autumn and winter cropping. Sow in mid-spring and transplant seedlings in early summer to their final spot.

2 Dwarf aubergines, such as 'Baby Rosanna', with its silvery green leaves and dark purple, glossy fruits, make attractive patio plants. Pot on (prick out) in pots that complement the colour of the flowers and fruits.

3 Aubergine blooms can be as attractive as that of any patio plant. Place the plants in a warm, sheltered spot and team up with tomato 'Totem' and baskets of cascading cherry tomatoes.

4 Dwarf purple French beans are grown in a similar way to runner beans (*see* page 81) but they only need a few twiggy sticks for support. The beans must be cooked before being eaten.

5 Many loose-leaf lettuce varieties (ones that don't make a solid heart) are quick to grow. Choose frilly red leaved types, such as 'Red Salad Bowl' and 'Delicato', for pretty edibles.

6 Radicchio, like lettuce, is easy to grow in pots and troughs. The red-tinged, mild outer leaves cover the dark red and white, strongly flavoured heart – the bit that's often added to salads.

 = Watch out! Sharp or dangerous tool in use. = Watch out! Adult help is needed.

7 The Swiss chard 'Bright Lights' has rainbow coloured stems. Add baby leaves to a plain green salad or ask an adult to help you cut larger leaves, which can be shredded, then steamed or stir-fried.

8 With their large blooms, big leaves and attractive fruits, cucurbits, such as courgettes, squashes and pumpkins, will put on a show when planted in a barrel.

TOP TIP

► Swiss chard can survive the winter if the crowns are protected with straw or a cloche (hot cap) in winter. Remove the protection in spring and mulch soil with manure.

Potato bin

A dustbin (trash can) might seem like a bizarre planter, but the black plastic heats up quickly and makes for speedy spud or potato growth – just what you want when growing delicious 'new' potatoes at the beginning of the season. Potatoes are actually swollen underground stems that the plant grows to store food in. By partially burying the plant, you force more potato tubers to form and a dustbin has plenty of depth. Put the lid back on overnight if frost is forecast.

you will need

- **seed potato tubers** (see Plant List)
- **egg boxes**
- **plastic dustbin (garbage can)**, 1
- **drill** with a **large drill bit** (for adult use only)
- **gravel**
- **peat-free potting compost** with **added loam (soil mix)**
- **slow-release fertilizer granules** (suitable for fruit and vegetables)
- **watering can**
- **soluble** or **liquid general fertilizer** (suitable for fruit and vegetables)
- **plastic sheet**

TOP TIP

► Provided your potatoes were disease-free, you can reuse the potting compost. Remove any roots and fill the new containers with the soil. Grow quick-maturing salads, such as radish, lettuce and round carrots. Or, keep it until autumn and use for bulb planting. Alternatively, refill the bin, add fertilizer and plant a trailing squash.

potatoes

plant list

✳ **Early and salad varieties of potato (*Solanum tuberosum*):**
'Anya'
'Charlotte'
'Lady Christi'
'Maris Bard'
'Rocket'
'Swift'
'Winston'

WARNING – All green parts of the potato plant are poisonous. Covering developing tubers with compost keeps them in the dark and stops them turning green.

1 Place seed potato tubers in egg boxes, with the end that has the most 'eyes' or buds uppermost. Place on a cool windowsill two weeks before you intend to plant out, and watch the shoots grow.

2 Once the tubers have sprouted, or 'chitted', prepare the dustbin by making drainage holes in the base. Ask an adult to drill these with a drill bit. Plastic potato-growing sacks (bags) are a patio alternative.

3 Ask an adult to help you pour 13cm/5in of gravel into the base of the dustbin. Add about 15cm/6in of potting compost mixed with some slow-release fertilizer.

4 Taking care not to damage the shoot grown from each potato (these are quite brittle), plant five tubers so that the shoot tips are just showing above the soil surface.

5 As the shoots grow, keep earthing-up (hilling up) the stems. That means adding more compost (5cm/2in at a time) to bury the lower stems. Water to keep the soil just moist.

 = Watch out! Sharp or dangerous tool in use. = Watch out! Adult help is needed.

6 Continue adding compost mixed with a little slow-release fertilizer until the soil level is almost at the top. Use additional fertilizer to boost growth when plants are growing well.

7 You'll know it is time to harvest when the flowers appear. These can be quite attractive. You may be able to harvest some potatoes from down the sides of the bin.

8 For the main harvest, spread out a plastic sheet and, with help, tip over the bin and shake the plants and soil out on to it. Delve into the soil and pull out all the tubers you find.

TOP TIP
▶ New potatoes are delicious boiled or steamed, cooled and mixed with mayonnaise and chopped chives or salad onions (scallions) for potato salad.

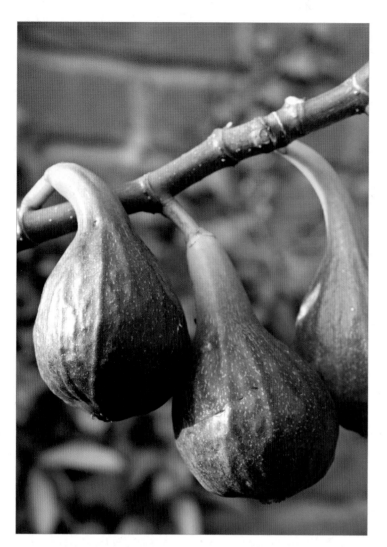

Fabulous figs

Figs can grow really big when planted in the ground, but are easier to manage and to get to fruit when grown in pots. They must have warmth and sunshine.

you will need
- **large terracotta pot**, 45–50cm/18–20in in diameter
- **crock** (clay piece) or **tile**
- **gravel**
- **trowel**
- **loam-based potting compost (soil mix)**, such as John Innes No. 3
- *Ficus carica* **'Brown Turkey'**, 1 plant
- **bucket** of **water**
- **watering can**
- **general-purpose liquid fertilizer**
- **liquid plant food**, such as tomato food

terracotta pot and compost

fig fruit and leaf

1 Cover the hole in the base of a pot with a crock or tile and ask an adult to help pour in about 2.5–5cm/1–2in gravel, or use a trowel.

2 Pour in a small quantity of potting compost. Meanwhile, soak the plant by plunging in a bucket of water until the bubbles stop.

3 Remove the fig from its pot and plant, adding more compost to fill in around the root-ball. Finish about 2½cm/1in below the rim of the pot. Water thoroughly with a watering can.

4 Feed weekly during spring and summer, alternating general-purpose fertilizer with tomato food.

5 Fruits ripen in autumn, turning golden or brown. They have very thin skins that sometimes start to split. The drooping figs pull off easily and should be eaten fresh.

6 After harvesting, pick off any fruits larger than marbles. Protect the plants from frost by putting them under cover.

bucket

TOP TIPS
▶ Ask an adult to help you prune the fig plant lightly in late winter using secateurs (pruners) to make an open shape. Remove dead wood in spring.
▶ Pinch summer-grown shoots back to 5–6 leaves in autumn.
▶ Wear gloves to keep the plant's sap off skin, as this may be an irritant when exposed to sunlight.

Blueberry bounty

A delicious treat, blueberries are irresistible to both humans and birds, so you need to be quick to pick them unless you cover the crop with netting!

you will need

- **blueberry bushes** (*see* Plant List), 2, different varieties
- **bucket** of **rainwater**
- **ceramic pots**, 2
- **crocks (clay pieces)**
- **gravel**
- **ericaceous (lime-free) potting compost**
- **trowel**
- **rainwater**
- **watering can**
- **ericaceous fertilizer**, such as rhododendron and azalea feed
- **larger tub** or **half-barrel**, 2, for potting on in second year
- **bamboo canes (stakes)**, 12
- **stiff wire** and **pliers** or **garden twine** and **scissors**
- **pea** and **bean netting**
- **clothes pegs (clothespins)**

plant list
❋ **Varieties of blueberry (*Vaccinium corymbosum*):**
'Patriot'

'Bluecrop'
'Bluegold'
'Blue Pearl'

1 Plunge the bushes in a bucket of rainwater, collected from a water butt (barrel), until the bubbles stop. You'll need two varieties for the best yield.

2 Cover the drainage holes in the pot with crocks and ask an adult to help you pour in about 2½cm/1in of gravel.

3 Add some ericaceous compost to the ceramic pots, using a trowel. Blueberries can't survive unless the soil and water used are lime-free.

4 Plant a blueberry bush in each of the prepared ceramic pots, firming the compost lightly around the roots.

5 Water the blueberry plants regularly with rainwater using a watering can. Feed every two weeks in the growing season with some ericaceous fertilizer (rhododendron and azalea feed), following the instructions on the packet.

6 Notice the fiery autumn leaf colour, which is a feature of blueberries. Pick off flower buds in the first spring.

7 Allow the plants to flower in the second year. Pot on (prick out) into larger tubs or half-barrels in the second year.

8 Before fruits ripen make a frame with three canes pushed into each tub or barrel. Connect the tops with three canes and join with wire or twine cut to length.

9 Drape the frame with netting, pulling it taut and attach with pegs. Leave an opening for picking fruit. Open and close with pegs.

Tasty hanging basket

All the ingredients for this basket have edible parts or fragrant flowers that can also be used as a garnish or food decoration, such as the pink, ball-shaped chive heads and purple-blue lavender spikes. Nasturtium blooms, sweet viola flowers and French marigold heads are edible too, as well as being insect attractors. Keep picking the parsley, chives, thyme and marjoram for the kitchen.

you will need

- **35cm/14in wire hanging basket**
- **heavy pot**
- **recycled wool, coir** or **natural-fibre basket liner**
- **assorted plants** (see Plant List)
- **moisture-retentive hanging basket compost (soil mix)**
- **bucket** of water
- **slow-releaser fertilizer granules**
- **watering can**

hanging basket

plant list

- ✳ **1 alpine strawberry/ frais des bois plant** *Fragaria vesca*
- ✳ **1 chive plant** *Allium schoenoprasum*
- ✳ **1 dwarf lavender plant** *Lavandula angustifolia* variety
- ✳ **4–5 French marigolds** *Tagetes patula*
- ✳ **1 golden marjoram plant** *Origanum vulgare* 'Aureum'
- ✳ **1 nasturtium** *Tropaeolum majus*
- ✳ **1 parsley plant** *Petroselinum crispum*
- ✳ **2 variegated thymes** *Thymus* 'Doone Valley'
- ✳ **4–5 violas** *Viola* Sorbet Series

alpine strawberries

1 Position a hanging basket in a pot. Unhook the chain and pull it to one side to give you room to work. Add a wool or coir basket liner. Plunge the plants in a bucket of water and wait for the bubbles to stop.

2 Half-fill the basket with moisture-retentive hanging basket compost, and plant the pot-grown nasturtium so that it trails over the edge of the basket. Plant two variegated thymes.

3 To make a pretty contrast to the orange nasturtium flowers, plant golden marjoram. This will form a spreading dome and will eventually cascade over the edge of the basket.

4 Violas have a sweet scent and are shade tolerant. Modern bedding types keep flowering for months if you deadhead them regularly. Plant little clumps between other low-growing herbs.

5 Keep the centre of the basket free so that you can plant a dwarf lavender as a specimen. Once this is in, add a chive plant. This can be split up in autumn or spring for more plants.

6 In the remaining space, squeeze in an alpine strawberry or frais des bois (strawberry of the woods). It's another shade-tolerant plant so won't mind being at the back.

 = Watch out! Sharp or dangerous tool in use. = Watch out! Adult help is needed.

7 In gaps between the basket plants, insert a few French marigolds. Deadhead regularly to keep them flowering. Ensure that you don't accidentally introduce tiny slugs or snails, which will eat them up!

8 If there's room, add parsley. Work in extra compost to fill the gaps between root-balls. Firm lightly. Reattach the chain and water thoroughly. Ask an adult to hang in a sunny spot.

TOP TIP

▶ To save planting space, you could sow nasturtium seeds into the compost. The seedlings will come up quickly and should flower well.

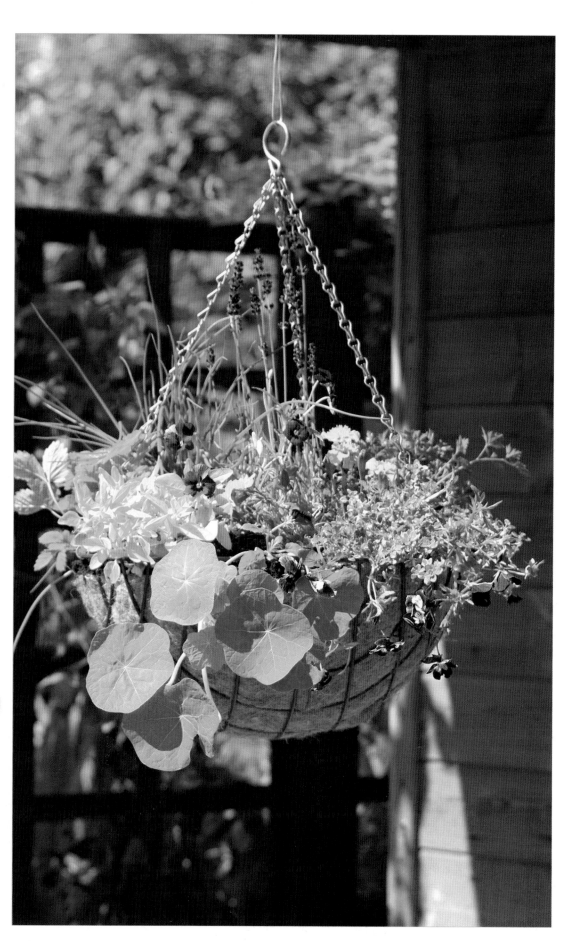

tasty hanging basket **65**

Minty madness

With so many to choose from, you could easily have over 20 types of mint in your collection in no time. They are easy to root in a jar of water and, once potted up, the baby plants make great presents for friends or family.

you will need

- **range** of **terracotta pots**, in different shapes and sizes
- **PVA (white) glue**
- **2½cm/1in paintbrush**, for applying glue
- **peppermint-coloured emulsion (latex) paint tester pot** or **acrylic paint**
- **artist's paintbrush**
- **selection** of **mint plants** (*see* Plant List)
- **bucket** of **water**
- **peat-free potting compost** with **added loam (soil mix)**
- **water-retaining gel crystals**
- **recycled plastic**
- **felt-tipped pen**
- **paints**
- **scissors**
- **wire**
- **waterproof adhesive tape**
- **watering can**
- **peppermint-coloured stone chips**

TOP TIP

► As well as smelling great, mints have a wide range of cosmetic, medicinal and culinary uses:

- Add apple mint leaves to summer fruit drinks or use sprigs to garnish desserts.
- Finely chop spearmint for mint sauce or sprinkle on to new potatoes.
- Use eau de Cologne mint to perfume bath water!

spearmint

plant list

- ✱ **Apple mint**
  Mentha suaveolens
- ✱ **Chocolate mint**
  Mentha x piperita f. *citrata* 'Chocolate'
- ✱ **Eau de Cologne mint**
  Mentha x piperita f. *citrata*
- ✱ **Lemon mint**
  Mentha piperita f. *citrata* 'Lemon'
- ✱ **Lime mint**
  Mentha piperita f. *citrata* 'Lime'
- ✱ **Pineapple mint**
  Mentha suaveolens 'Variegata'
- ✱ **Red mint**
  Mentha X *smithiana*
- ✱ **Silver mint**
  Mentha longifolia
- ✱ **Spearmint (garden mint)**
  Mentha spicata

eau de Cologne mint

apple mint

1 Paint all the pots with a dilute solution of PVA glue using a 2½cm/1in paintbrush. Paint peppermint-coloured stripes on to the pots using an artist's paintbrush, to emphasize the mint theme.

2 It is essential that broad-leaved mints don't run short of moisture, as this can lead to mildew. To prevent this, plunge the plants in a bucket and wait for the bubbles to stop.

3 Mix the compost with water-retaining gel crystals, then put some into the pots and plant the mints. As they grow you'll need to divide them or pot them on into larger containers.

4 Fill in down the sides of the root-balls with compost and firm lightly, leaving a gap between the surface of the root-ball and the pot rim for watering. Smell the leaves as you work.

 = Watch out! Sharp or dangerous tool in use. = Watch out! Adult help is needed.

5 A fun way to remember what all of the mints in your collection are called is to make labels that give you a clue. Draw on to recycled plastic using a felt-tipped pen, then paint.

6 Cut out the labels (adult supervision is required). Attach to wire with waterproof adhesive tape. Position the labels when dry. Here, a pineapple represents pineapple mint.

7 Ensure the pots are well watered, then group the mints in a lightly shaded corner and finish off the display by pouring peppermint-coloured stone chips around the base.

TOP TIP
▶ Mints tend to have a bad reputation for spreading if planted in the ground, so growing them in pots is a way to help control their rampant nature.

Going bananas!

With their giant leaves, bananas add a tropical touch to your garden. The little plants you buy in garden centres can grow to 1.8m/6ft. They may not produce fruit, but still look impressive.

you will need

- **young banana plant** (see Plant List), 1
- **bucket** of **water**
- **crocks** (clay pieces)
- **patio pots**, various sizes
- **gravel**
- **peat-free potting compost** (soil mix)
- **trowel**
- **watering can**
- **soluble plant food**
- **cobbles** or **ornamental bark**, for decoration

cobbles

plant list

✱ **Patio varieties of banana:**
Ensete ventricosum
Ensete ventricosum 'Maurelii'

Musa acuminata 'Zebrina'
Musa basjoo
Musa sikkimensis

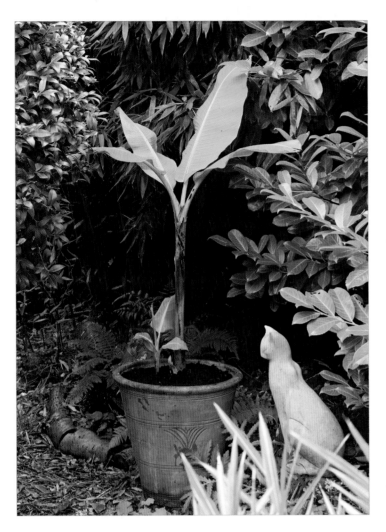

1 Choose a sheltered spot outside. Plunge the plant in a bucket of water until the bubbles stop.

2 Put some crocks in the bottom of a patio pot and add a layer of gravel for drainage. Three-quarters fill the pot with compost, then make a hole with a trowel and plant the banana plant.

3 Water the plant regularly and feed following instructions on the packet.

4 Pot into a larger container as needed, to keep pace with the stem and leaf growth. Eventually, your banana can go in a really big pot, as shown – ask an adult to help with any lifting.

5 Top the pot with cobbles or ornamental bark. When suckers develop at the base, you can grow a new banana plant by cutting it off with a knife (ask an adult to help) and potting it up.

banana

TOP TIP

▶ In winter, either move the plant into a conservatory (sun room) or insulate the pot with bubble wrap, top the compost with 10cm/4in bark and wrap the main stem with hessian (burlap) sacks filled with straw. The leaves may die but the plant should re-shoot.

(!) = Watch out! Sharp or dangerous tool in use.   = Watch out! Adult help is needed.

Runner bean wigwam

Originally introduced for their pretty flowers, runner beans also produce an abundance of tasty, tender and nutritious pods if the plants are kept well fed and watered – yummy!

you will need

- **digging fork** or **spade**
- **well-rotted manure**
- **2.4m/8ft bamboo canes (stakes)**, 5
- **step ladder**
- **garden twine**
- **scissors**
- **small pots** and **compost**
- **bean seeds** (see Plant List)
- **watering can**

plant list
Recommended varieties of runner bean (Phaseolus coccineus):
'Desiree'
'Galaxy'
'Mergoles'
'Painted Lady'

runner beans, leaves and flowers

1 Dig over a section of flower border or vegetable garden and work in some well-rotted manure. Adult help may be required. This will keep the beans moist.

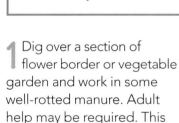

2 Push five long bamboo canes into the ground, making a circle about 1m/3ft across. Ask an adult to help if you find this difficult.

3 Standing on a step ladder if necessary (ask an adult to help you), tie the canes together at the top with garden twine to make a wigwam (tepee).

4 Fill some small pots with compost and plant a bean per pot to grow on a windowsill, in case the ones outside don't grow properly or get eaten!

5 Outside, make a hole on each side of the cane about 3cm/1¼in deep. Put one bean in each hole.

6 Water during dry weather and protect from slugs (see page 41). When they reach the top of the wigwam, pinch out the shoot tips. Don't allow pods to mature fully or bean production will stop.

TOP TIP
► Another way to ensure that bean roots have all the moisture they need is to dig a deeper planting hole, fill it with shredded recycled newspaper, grass cuttings and garden compost, water, then put the soil back on top.

Herb wheel

A herb garden makes an attractive feature in a small vegetable plot or a sunny area of gravel. If you leave herbs to flower they attract pollinating insects, but this makes the foliage of edible kinds less tasty. A compromise is to plant two of each type, letting one flower while the other one is grown purely for picking.

you will need

- **border fork**
- **grit**, optional
- **garden compost**, optional
- **wooden wagon wheel** or **bricks**
- **loam-based potting compost (soil mx)** or **soil**
- **range** of **herbs** (*see* Plant List)
- **bucket of water**
- **trowel**
- **hand brush**
- **20cm/8in terracotta pot**
- **horticultural grit**
- **watering can**

plant list

- ✳ **Chives**
  Allium schoenoprasum
- ✳ **Cotton lavender (lavender cotton)**
  Santolina chamaecyparissus
- ✳ **Dwarf English lavender**
  Lavandula angustifolia variety
- ✳ **Gold variegated sage**
  Salvia officinalis 'Icterina'
- ✳ **Golden thyme**
  Thymus pulegioides 'Bertram Anderson'
- ✳ **Hyssop**
  Hyssopus officinalis
- ✳ **Moss curled parsley**
  Petroselinum crispum
- ✳ **Pineapple mint**
  Mentha suaveolens 'Variegata'

- ✳ **Purple sage**
  Salvia officinalis 'Purpurascens'
- ✳ **Rosemary**
  Rosmarinus officinalis
- ✳ **Variegated marjoram**
  Origanum vulgare 'Country Cream', 'Gold Tip'
- ✳ **Variegated thyme**
  Thymus 'Doone Valley'

gold variegated sage

rosemary

1 Dig over the area chosen for the wheel using a border fork. Break up any large clumps of soil to improve drainage. Fork in grit and garden compost if the soil is a heavy clay type. Adult supervision is required.

2 Level the ground and ask an adult to help you position the wagon wheel. This provides planting pockets that keep the plants separate. If you can't get one, ask an adult to help you make a replica out of bricks.

3 Fill in the empty wheel sections with loam-based potting compost or soil. This will give the young plants a chance to root freely. Firm lightly and level off with your hands.

4 Plunge the herbs in a bucket of water and wait for the bubbles to stop. Use a trowel to make holes. Plant the golden thyme, cream variegated marjoram and purple sage.

5 Continue, placing the herbs to create as much contrast in colour, leaf shape and texture as possible. Plant the parsley, yellow variegated marjoram, cotton lavender and variegated thyme.

6 Plant the chives and yellow variegated sage. Finish with hyssop, the variegated mint and lavender. Firm in the herbs. Using a hand brush, sweep excess soil from the wheel.

7 Plant a small rosemary plant in a 20cm/8in terracotta pot filled with a gritty soil mix. Place the pot in the centre of the wheel to act as a focal point. You could also use lavender or a bay tree.

8 Add a layer of horticultural grit to the surface of the compost in the rosemary pot. It will help to highlight the foliage and keep the neck of the plant dry. Water the wheel.

TOP TIP

▶ To keep your plants healthy, pick the leaves and soft stems of the edible kinds frequently, especially chives, parsley and mint.

herb wheel   **71**

Chequerboard plot

If you only have a little corner to garden in, then dividing it up into squares can help you make the most of the space. Choose dwarf and compact vegetable and herb varieties, which will crop in a very small space and won't grow so tall that they overshadow their neighbours. Keep a note of what you sow in each of the squares so that you remember to sow or plant vegetables from different groups the following season.

you will need

- **border fork**
- **wheelbarrow**
- **manure** (at least 3 years old) or **garden compost**
- **slow-release fertilizer granules**, for edible plants
- **1.2m/4ft canes (stakes)**, 8–10
- **tape measure** or **ruler**
- **garden twine**
- **scissors**
- **trowel** or **dibber (dibble)**
- **assorted plants** (see Plant List)
- **bucket** of **water**
- **recycled plastic bottle cloche(s)** (see page 41)
- **fleece** (floating row cover)
- **watering can**

plant list

* **Baby beetroot (beet)**
  Beta vulgaris 'Boltardy'
* **Common thyme**
  Thymus serpyllum
* **Compact cabbage**
  Brassica oleracea var. capitata 'Golden Acre'
* **Dwarf broad (fava) bean**
  Vicia faba 'The Sutton'
* **Dwarf curly kale**
  Brassica oleracea var. acephala 'Starbor' F1
* **Dwarf pea**
  Pisum sativum 'Little Marvel'
* **Garlic chives**
  Allium tuberosum

* **Lettuce**
  Lactuca sativa 'Little Gem'
* **Mini courgette (zucchini)**
  Cucurbita pepo 'Bambino' F1
* **Radicchio**
  Cichorium intybus
* **Round carrot**
  Daucus carota 'Parmex'
* **Salad onion (scallion)**
  Allium cepa 'White Lisbon'
* **Radish**
  Raphanus sativus 'Cherry Belle'
* **Viola**
  Viola Sorbet Series

TOP TIPS

▶ 1.2m/4ft wide raised beds (shown here) are perfect for growing vegetables, especially on poor ground with thin soil or where the ground is heavy and poorly drained. Fill the space created by the raised edges with soil, garden compost and manure.

▶ You don't have to dig to cultivate, just keep beds filled up with compost.

▶ You can easily work from the edges of the raised area, which stops the beds getting compacted.

1 Fork a wheelbarrow load of manure or garden compost into the area you are going to cultivate. Adult help may be required. This is important if the ground had crops on it last year.

2 Add some slow-release fertilizer to give plants a steady supply of feed. Peas and beans are able to make their own fertilizer and they leave nutrients in the soil after they die down.

3 Lay out four 1.2m/4ft bamboo canes and use a tape measure or ruler to set them 30cm/12in apart. If you like, you can make the squares slightly larger or lay them out differently.

4 Place the set of vertical canes down on top of the horizontal ones, set out at the same distance apart. Use garden twine to join the canes together where they cross.

5 Use a trowel or a dibber to make planting holes for seedlings and plantlets. Soak the various plants before planting out by plunging them in a bucket of water until the bubbles stop.

6 As well as planting home-grown seedlings and strips of vegetable plants bought from garden centres, sow quick-maturing salad seeds, such as lettuce. You don't have to sow in rows.

7 Plant flowers, such as violas, in some of the squares to attract pollinating bees and beneficial insects, which can help control pests. Pot marigolds are also a good choice.

8 Use plastic bottles as cloches (hot caps) to protect seedlings from cold and slugs. Surround carrots with fleece to keep off carrot fly. Water plants often during warm weather.

Beautiful blooms

Here you will find how to grow a wide variety of colourful and fragrant flowers to brighten your garden, at the same time giving bees and other beneficial insects a treat. There are quirky containers for growing pretty or scented plants, and as well as potted patio ideas and border displays there are fun dried-flower and bulb-planting projects

Pots of flowers

Sow quick-and-easy hardy annual flowers in pots to brighten up dull parts of the garden, such as a driveway or paved area.

you will need

- large, **colourful plastic containers** or **planters**
- **utility knife** (for adult use only)
- **colour-coordinated hardy annual seed mixtures** (see Plant List)
- **trowel** or **dustpan**
- **gravel**
- **peat-free potting compost** with **added loam (soil mix)**
- **watering can** with a **fine rose (sprinkler) attachment**
- **horticultural grit**

horticultural grit

plant list

- ✳ **Californian poppy**
  Eschscholzia c alifornica
- ✳ **Clarkia**
  Clarkia elegans
- ✳ **Cornflower**
  Centaurea cyanus
- ✳ **Godetia**
  Godetia grandiflora
- ✳ **Love-in-a-mist**, **devil in the bush**
  Nigella damascena

- ✳ **Mallow**
  Lavatera trimestris
- ✳ **Mallow-wort**, **mallope**
  Malope trifida
- ✳ **Poached egg plant**
  Limnanthes douglasii
- ✳ **Pot marigold**
  Calendula officinalis
- ✳ **Shirley poppy**
  Papaver rhoeas Shirley Series
- ✳ **Tickseed**
  Coreopsis tinctoria

1 Ask an adult to cut a few pieces out of the base of each container using a utility knife, if necessary. Without holes, water makes the compost soggy and will drown the plant roots.

2 Choose seeds to go in coloured containers. We've used a red mix to go in an orange one and an orange mix to go in a purple one.

3 Using a trowel or dustpan, pour several centimetres (inches) of gravel into the bottom of each tub, then fill with compost and water well. Adult help may be required.

4 Sow by pouring the seeds out on to the flat of your hand. You will see that there are small and large seeds.

5 Space out a selection of the larger seeds on the surface of the compost (each flower has a differently shaped seed).

6 Scatter the smaller seeds thinly between the larger ones. You will probably have enough seeds for two tubs and dividing the seeds will help prevent sowing too thickly.

7 Cover the seeds with a thin layer of grit, using a dustpan. The tiny seedlings will soon appear. Water as required.

mallow

marigold

 = Watch out! Sharp or dangerous tool in use. = Watch out! Adult help is needed.

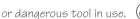

Giant dahlia

Dahlias are show-offs! Tall, big and colourful, they will give your garden or patio a totally tropical feel!

you will need

- **dahlia tuber** (*see* Plant List)
- **small seed tray**
- **soil-less seed** and **cutting compost (soil mix)** with added **Perlite**
- **25cm/10in pot**
- **peat-free potting compost** with added **loam (soil mix)**
- **watering can**
- **bamboo canes (stakes)** (various sizes)
- **soft garden twine**
- **grit** or **fine gravel**
- **clay pots**, (5cm/10in, 5cm/14in and 40cm/16in in diameter, for potting on)
- **crocks (clay pieces)**, for potting on
- **gravel**, for potting on
- **general flowering plant liquid fertilizer**
- **liquid tomato food**

plant list
✳ **Tall large-flowered types of dahlia (*Dahlia*):**
'Admiral Rawlings'
'Café au Lait'
'Gallery Art Nouveau'
'Grenadier'
'Kenora Sunset'
'Kidd's Climax'
'Zorro'

1 Put the tuber into a seed tray filled with slightly moist seed and cutting compost to start the tuber growing and plump it up. Keep on a windowsill or in a frost-free greenhouse until it sprouts green shoots.

2 Plant the tuber in a 25cm/10in pot so that the shoots are just poking up through the compost.

3 Alternatively, plant the tuber halfway down the pot to start with and keep adding compost as the shoots grow (but don't bury the tips).

4 As it gets bigger in late spring, start to harden it off, putting outdoors for a few hours a day. Or, use a cold frame and increase ventilation gradually (see page 13).

5 Put a cane into the pot to support the growing plant. You will need to replace this with a taller cane as the plant grows. Tie the stem on gently using soft garden twine.

6 Pinch out the main shoot tip with your thumb and index finger as the plant grows to encourage side branches.

7 Water and cover the compost with grit. This helps stop slugs and snails eating the plant.

8 Continue watering and feed with general liquid fertilizer. Pot on (prick out) into progressively larger pots when the roots start to poke out of the drainage hole. Switch to tomato food when the plant begins flowering.

Flowering boots

When you have grown out of a pair of Wellington boots, why not turn them into fun containers for plants? You just need to create a few drainage holes, fill them with soil and plant away!

you will need

- **wellington (rubber) boots**, 1 pair
- **utility knife** (adult use only)
- **trowel**
- **gravel**
- **peat-free potting compost** with **added loam (soil mix)**
- **plants** (see Plant List)
- **bucket** of **water**
- **watering can**

plant list

Summer

* **Swan river daisy**
  Brachyscome multifida
* **Trailing geranium**
  Pelargonium cvs.
* **Trailing petunia**
  Petunia Surfinia Baby Pink Morn
* **Twin spur**
  Diascia 'Ruby Field'

Winter/Spring

* **Double daisy**
  Bellis perennis
* **Dwarf daffodil**
  Narcissus 'Tête-à-tête'
* **Hardy primrose**
  Primula Wanda hybrids
* **Mini cyclamen**
  Cyclamen Miracle Series

1 Ask an adult to cut a few small holes round the base of the boots, using a utility knife. Cut the holes just above the thick sole of the wellington boots to provide drainage. It is a good idea to rest the boots on an upturned pot to cut the holes.

2 Using a trowel, fill the foot of the boots with gravel for drainage and to stop the boot falling over.

3 Next add compost to the boots. You'll need to work it well into the foot and ankle parts of the boots with your hand.

4 Plunge the plants in a bucket of water until the bubbles stop. Remove from their pots.

5 Carefully lower the plant in the top of the boots. There should be enough compost to support the plant at the right height.

6 Add more compost to fill the gaps around the root-ball, then firm in.

7 Stand the boots in a sheltered spot out of direct sun. Water cyclamen under the leaves, only when the compost feels a little dry.

Bags of blooms

These plastic-coated canvas shopping bags are great as plant containers for the summer. You'll find them in all shapes, sizes, colours and patterns. These have a different pirate picture on opposite sides.

you will need

- **plastic-coated canvas shopping bags**, 2
- **scissors**
- **bedding** or **patio plants** (*see* Plant List), enough to fill the bags
- **bucket** of **water**
- **peat-free potting compost** with **added loam (soil mix)**
- **trowel**
- **watering can**

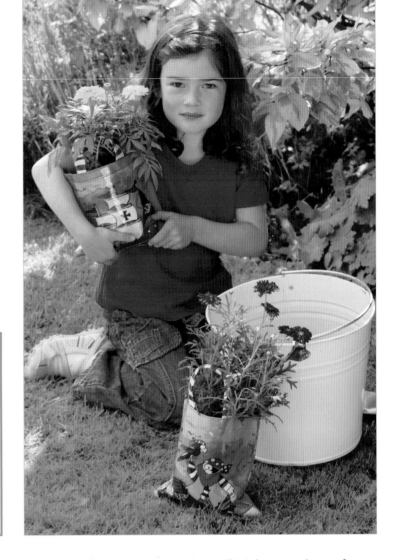

plant list

- ❋ **African marigold**
  Tagetes erecta 'French Vanilla'
- ❋ **Bidens**
  Bidens ferulifolia
- ❋ **Busy Lizzie**
  Impatiens Accent Series
- ❋ **Fibrous-rooted begonia**
  Begonia sempervirens
- ❋ **French marigold**
  Tagetes patula
- ❋ **Geranium**
  Pelargonium (Zonal)
- ❋ **Trailing verbena**
  Verbena Tapien Series

* Nip off the faded flowers to keep plants blooming.

1 Ask an adult to help you cut out two or three small holes in the bottom of each bag using scissors. This will allow excess water to run out.

2 Plunge the plants in a bucket of water until the bubbles stop.

3 Half-fill each bag with potting compost using a trowel.

4 Leave enough room for the root-balls to be planted (try them in the bags for size). Allow a few centimetres/inches free at the top for watering.

5 Take the soaked plants (here a marigold) out of their pots and position in each of the bags.

6 Fill the gaps round the roots of the plants with more potting compost and firm in lightly using your fingers.

7 Make sure the surface of the root-ball is just covered but don't pile soil up round the neck of the plant or bury any leaves. Water with a watering can.

TOP TIP
▶ To help keep larger bags upright, add several centimetres/inches of gravel.

Potted perfumes

Fragrance makes being out in the garden even more enjoyable. A collection of perfumed flowers and herbs is a particularly nice idea for a sitting area. Of course, there are many more scented plants than those used here. Make a point of smelling flowers that you come across and try to describe what they are like and if they remind you of other things, such as lemons or apples.

you will need
- **assorted fragrant plants** (see Plant List)
- **bucket** of **water**
- **animal-shaped terracotta planters,** 2
- **loam-based potting compost** (soil mix)
- **trowel**
- **terracotta bowl**
- **crock (clay piece)**
- **gravel**
- **horticultural grit**
- **watering can**
- **assorted pots**

variegated apple mint

FACT FILE

SCENTS AND AROMAS

Plants use fragrance to attract insects such as bees, butterflies and moths. The clove-scented pinks featured here have a sweet, spicy fragrance that is easy to smell on a warm, still day. To pick up the scent of aromatic herbs such as thyme, apple mint and lavender, rub the leaves between your fingers.

lavender

pink

plant list
* **2 clove-scented pinks**
  Dianthus
* **3 dwarf English lavenders**
  Lavandula angustifolia 'Hidcote'
* **2 French lavenders**
  Lavandula pedunculata subsp. *pedunculata*
* **2 thymes**
  Thymus pulegioides
* **1 variegated apple mint**
  Mentha suaveolens 'Variegata'

1 Plunge all the plants in a bucket of water until the bubbles stop. This ensures that the compost is moist through to the middle. Take the first clove-scented pink from its pot.

2 Unlike glazed or plastic-lined pots, the terracotta cat planters we used are small and porous so won't need extra drainage. Add a little compost with a trowel.

3 Position the pink on the compost, in the centre, then add extra compost as required to fill any gaps round the edges, leaving a small gap for watering. Firm in lightly.

4 Choose a pink with a different petal colour and pattern from the one you have just planted and plant in the second container, repeating the method described.

 = Watch out! Sharp or dangerous tool in use.   = Watch out! Adult help is needed.

5 Next, prepare a terracotta bowl for planting by covering the drainage hole with a crock and adding some gravel with a trowel to ensure good drainage.

6 Add compost. Most herbs hate getting too damp so add grit to the compost if you use a glazed pot. This terracotta one will lose moisture through the sides so won't get too damp.

7 Remove the lavender from its plastic pot and plant it in the bowl. The surface of the root-ball should be just under the lip of the bowl to allow space for watering.

8 Add two more plants, then fill in the gaps with compost, and water. Continue planting up other plants. Thyme grows well in terracotta pots but use a glazed container for mint.

Everlasting flowers

Dried flowers make long-lasting arrangements. You can dry any blooms, but ones that are naturally dry or papery are especially suitable.

you will need
- scissors
- garden twine
- hammer
- nail or hook
- vase, (optional)

plant list
- **Big quaking grass**
  Briza maxima
- **Globe thistle**
  Echinops ritro
- **Lavender**
  Lavandula spp. and varieties
- **Masterwort**
  Astrantia major
- **Ornamental grasses**
  Miscanthus
- **Pearly everlasting**
  Anaphalis triplinervis
- **Statice, wavyleaf sea lavender**
  Limonium sinuatum
- **Sea holly**
  Eryngium spp. and varieties
- **Strawflower**
  Bracteantha bracteata
- **Yarrow**
  Achillea millefolium

1 Pick a dry day when the dew has disappeared. Using scissors, cut flowers with long stems. Adult supervision is required.

2 Prepare the separate bunches of flowers by removing all the foliage and clustering the flower heads together. Cut the stems to the same length.

3 Tightly tie each bundle with garden twine. The stems will shrink as they dry and may come loose otherwise. Leave a long piece for hanging.

4 Find a cool, dry, airy place for hanging the bunches. You may need to ask an adult to hammer in a nail or hook.

5 Hang up the bunch of flowers by the long piece of twine you left loose.

6 Depending on how large and full of moisture the flowers are when you cut them, it could take several weeks before they are dry enough to take down to arrange in a vase or hang up indoors or outside.

TOP TIP
▶ Try to pick perfect flowers for drying. Ones that aren't fully open work best because flowers continue to develop during the drying process and may drop their petals. Fully dry flowers are firm and unyielding.

 = Watch out! Sharp or dangerous tool in use.   = Watch out! Adult help is needed.

Spring drift

Seeing bulbs pushing their way through the ground lets you know that spring is on its way. Plant early varieties in a lawn to create a cheerful scene.

crocus

you will need
- **spring bulbs** (see Plant List) at least 2 large packets
- **bulb planter**, preferably long-handled

plant list
- ✳ **Daffodils**
  Narcissus cvs.
- ✳ **Drooping star of Bethlehem**
  Ornithogalum nutans
- ✳ **'Dutch' crocuses**
  Crocus vernus types
- ✳ **Early yellow crocus**
  Crocus × *luteus* 'Golden Yellow'
- ✳ **Grape hyacinths**
  Muscari armeniacum
- ✳ **Siberian squill**
  Scilla siberica
- ✳ **Snakeshead fritillaries**
  Fritillaria meleagris
- ✳ **Snowdrops**
  Galanthus nivalis
- ✳ **Species crocus**
  Crocus tommasinianus

1 Take handfuls of bulbs and throw them randomly on to the lawn.

2 Using a long-handled bulb planter, make holes of an appropriate depth for each bulb. The hole should be 2½–3 times deeper than the length of the bulb. You may need to ask an adult to help you.

3 As you work, the bulb planter will squeeze out a circular plug of turf and soil taken from the previous hole. Hold the plug to one side and put a bulb in the hole.

4 Replace the turf plug, and continue making holes and planting with all the bulbs.

5 Lightly tread the turf plugs back into position to leave the lawn level.

6 After the crocuses have flowered in spring, water in liquid tomato food and then allow about six weeks for the leaves to die down before mowing. The bulbs then build reserves for next year's display.

TOP TIP
▶ When planting larger bulbs in a lawn, rather than planting them individually, lift patches of turf with a spade. Loosen the bottom of the hole with a border fork, plant the bulbs, then replace the turf. Adult supervision is required.

Little and large sunflowers

Cheap to buy and fun to grow, you could have a competition to see which of your family or friends can grow the tallest sunflower? Some, such as 'Russian Giant', will tower over you, reaching 2.4m/8ft or more. To get a head start, grow several seedlings and select only the tallest and strongest-looking ones.

you will need
- **trowel** (optional)
- **8cm/3in plant pots** or **yogurt containers**
- **peat-free seed** and **cuttings compost**
- **dibber (dibble)** or **bamboo cane (stake)**
- **sunflower seeds** (see Plant List)
- **tray of water**
- **plastic bags**
- **ties**
- **13cm/5in pots**
- **peat-free compost** with **added loam (soil mix)**
- **old fork**
- **watering can** with a **fine rose (sprinkler head) attachment**
- **flowering plant food**

FACT FILE
BIRD FOOD
Tall, large-flowered sunflowers make tasty treats for seed-eating birds, such as finches, if they are left to produce seed-heads. Once the seed has ripened, you can either leave the heads on the dying stems or cut them off and hang them from the bird table using wire.

sunflower

plant list
✳ **Dwarf sunflowers** (*Helianthus annuus*):
  'Big Smile'
  'Dwarf Yellow Spray'
  'Little Dorrit'

✳ **Tall sunflowers** (*Helianthus annuus*):
  'Moonwalker'
  'Russian Giant'

1 Using a trowel or your hands, fill 8cm/3in plant pots or yogurt containers with seed compost and firm the compost lightly with your fingers.

2 Use a dibber or cane to make a hole 1.5cm/½in) deep. Repeat with the other pots.

3 Sow the seeds, then cover with compost. Stand in a tray of water until the compost darkens.

4 Cover with the plastic bags, tied at the top to act like a mini greenhouse. Grow on a windowsill. Remove the covers once the seedlings appear.

5 When the seedlings develop two or three pairs of leaves, they need potting on (pricking out).

6 Half-fill 13cm/5in pots with potting compost. Ease the seedlings out of their pots using an old fork. Hold the seedlings by a leaf and support the roots.

7 Position the seedlings gently in the centre of the larger pots, adding enough compost to cover the roots.

8 The seedlings should be planted at the same depth in the bigger pots as they were when they were in the smaller pots.

(!) = Watch out! Sharp or dangerous tool in use.   = Watch out! Adult help is needed

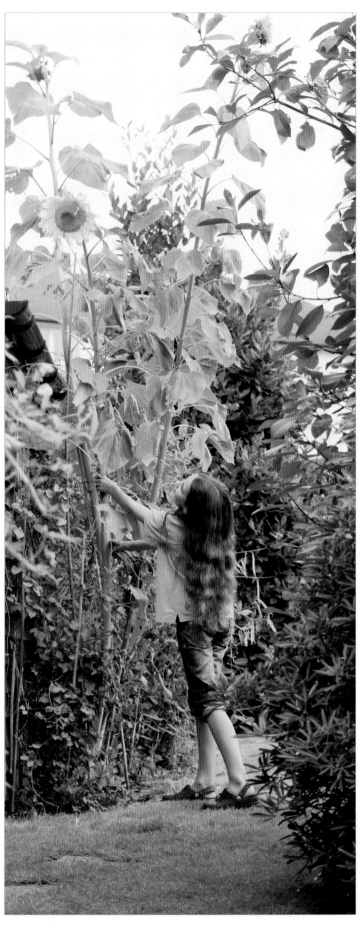

11 Pinch out the growing tip of dwarf types when they have five pairs of leaves to encourage side shoots.

9 Firm in lightly with your fingers and then water the seedlings with a watering can fitted with a rose attachment.

10 Grow on plants in a warm, sunny place, gradually hardening them off as the weather warms up (*see* page 13).

12 Plant dwarf varieties in pots and tall ones in borders, where they need support. Water often and feed once every two weeks with flowering plant food.

Autumn rainbow

This rainbow-like feature is planted with late summer and autumn plants for instant effect and will last until the first hard frost. You could also do a summer version. If you are happy to wait a few weeks for flowers to appear, save money by using young bedding plants.

you will need
- border fork
- garden rake
- slow-release fertilizer granules
- **plant selection** (see Plant List)
- **bucket** of **water**
- trowel
- border spade (optional)
- **watering can** with a **fine rose (sprinkler) attachment**

garden rake

FACT FILE
PRETTY BUT POISONOUS!
The orange-berried winter cherry included here is grown purely for decoration. Like many of its relatives, it is poisonous to eat. Its family, the *Solanaceae*, includes some familiar fruit and veg – potato, tomato, aubergine (eggplant), sweet pepper and chilli pepper. **Never eat anything unless an adult has told you that it is safe to do so!**

winter cherry

plant list
* **Autumn bedding viola**
  Viola Sorbet Series
* **Busy Lizzie**
  Impatiens New Guinea hybrids
* **Dwarf Michaelmas daisy**
  Aster novi-belgii cvs.
* **Heather**
  Calluna vulgaris (blue-dyed)
* **Winter cherry**
  Solanum pseudocapsicum
  (poisonous!)

WARNING – The winter cherry fruits are poisonous if eaten! You could use orange mini chrysanthemums, autumn crop pot marigolds (*Calendula*) or orange violas as alternatives.

1 Fork over the earth, then rake in some slow-release fertilizer, following packet instructions. Adult supervision is required. Plunge the plants in a bucket of water until the bubbles stop. Dig holes in an arc and plant the violas.

2 Alternatively, ask an adult to help you dig a shallow, curved trench with a spade and, after removing the pots, place all the violas in together. Draw soil dug out from the hole or trench back around the plant roots.

3 Take care to gently feel for gaps around the plants with your fingers and work the soil in between. Firm the soil lightly with the flat of your hand. Repeat for the rest of the violas so they are all firmed in.

4 Set out the next row of plants. In this case we've chosen orange-berried winter cherry (*see* Fact File and the Plant List). You won't need as many of these plants as the small bedding violas.

 = Watch out! Sharp or dangerous tool in use.   = Watch out! Adult help is needed.

5 After planting the winter cherry, add a row of the red, large-flowered busy Lizzie plants from the New Guinea hybrid group. For a hardier alternative, plant a staggered double row of scarlet red mini cyclamen.

6 Settle the soil after planting the busy Lizzies, then plant a staggered row of blue-dyed heathers. The dye is harmless and eventually fades! Leave enough room for a few purple flowers.

7 Select a range of lilac and violet-blue mini Michaelmas daisies to plant between the red busy Lizzies and blue heathers. Finish planting all the remaining rainbow flowers. Water in well.

VARIATION
• Use the following plants to make a summer rainbow: French marigolds, pot marigolds, bedding salvias, swan river daisies and ornamental sage.

Wildlife gardens

This chapter reveals different ways to discover more about the creatures that share our gardens and how to encourage them to stick around. You can make habitats for all kinds of animal life, both large and small, as well as feeding stations and even places for them to nest or hibernate. So, get planting, and your garden will soon be buzzing!

Backyard safari

There's no need to travel to exotic places looking for wildlife – your backyard is full of exciting creatures and minibeasts! Use an old can or jar to hold creatures safely while you investigate them with a magnifying glass, but remember to return them to their homes afterwards. Adult supervision is required, and great care should be taken if potentially harmful animals could be near.

you will need
- **magnifying glass** or **hand lens**
- **notebook**
- **pencil**
- **camera**
- **binoculars**
- **guidebook** or **wildlife identification sheets**

magnifying glass

FACT FILE
ON THE SNAIL TRAIL
Garden snails and slugs are nocturnal, living in cool shade. They eat flowers, leaves, fruit and decaying matter. Slime or mucus allows them to travel over rough surfaces. In autumn, snails hibernate, sealing up their shells. The fastest snails are speckled garden ones, which can move up to 55m/55yd per hour, while other land snails only move at about 60cm/24in in an hour.

garden snail

WILDLIFE WISE
Although many animals that are found in gardens are harmless, some may not be. Do not touch anything unless an adult says you can, and take extra care if you know there are any dangerous creatures where you live. Adult supervision is always required.

1 Carefully lift stones and pebbles and slates to see what animals are hiding underneath. It's best not to lift small creatures as you might crush them. Afterwards, put the stone back as it was.

2 Use a magnifying glass to find out about the creatures you find. What shape, size and colour are they? How many legs can you see? Try drawing the animal or take a picture.

3 Rotten logs and tree stumps are great places to look for minibeasts. Search under pieces of loose bark. You may find tunnels and boreholes left by burrowing worms and larvae.

4 There are many kinds of spider living in the garden. See how many species you can find and make a note of where you find them. Some have beautiful markings and make intricate webs.

 = Watch out! Sharp or dangerous tool in use. = Watch out! Adult help is needed.

5 Some creatures, such as beetles and ants, quickly run for cover when disturbed. Others, such as slugs, snails, caterpillars and woodlice, move slowly, allowing you to observe them quite easily.

6 A pair of binoculars is useful for looking at birds and larger animals, such as squirrels, especially those sitting up high. Keep yourself hidden from view, still and quiet.

7 Butterfly and other wildlife identification sheets are really useful for working out what you are looking at. Choose one that is suitable for the area you live in.

8 If you come across a nest, such as this robin's nest, in long grass, be very careful not to disturb it. Do not touch it as your smell could scare birds off!

Feed the birds

Help the birds that live in or pass through your garden by putting out a range of foods for them. Different birds are adapted to eat certain types: some have fine beaks designed for eating worms and insects; others, such as finches, have stout, seed-crushing beaks. Birds get used to knowing they have food, so keep putting it out!

you will need
- **assorted bird food** (see Fact File)
- **ground feeder tray** or **bird table**
- **fat ball hanger**
- **peanut feeder**
- **mixed seed feeder**
- **niger seed feeder**
- **container**
- **bottle brush**
- **scrubbing brush**
- **mild detergent**

FACT FILE

WHAT'S ON THE MENU?

- **Mealworms** These freeze-dried grubs can be used dry or soaked in warm water for 15 minutes.
- **Fat snacks** A blend of fat and mixed seed wrapped in mesh, fat snacks can be hung on twigs or from special feeders.
- **Black sunflower seeds** Black sunflower seeds won't swell up with water and block feeders.

mealworms

fat snacks

black sunflower seeds

- **Peanuts** These are a great source of fat and protein. Don't put whole nuts on a bird table during the nesting season as baby birds can choke.
- **Niger seed** Rich in oil, this is a favourite food of goldfinches. Use with a special feeder.
- **Mixed seed** Supply this general food in hanging feeders or on bird tables.

peanuts

niger seed

mixed seed

1 Some birds are more comfortable feeding on the ground but to keep food clean and contained, use a ground feeder tray that has a fine mesh, which allows water to drain through.

2 Site trays and bird tables in a relatively open area away from bushes where predators can lie in wait. They do also require some cover to retreat to if danger threatens.

3 Hanging feeders are used by relatively agile birds that can grip the sides. A variety of fat snack feeders is available. Hang from pergolas, archways and trellis or in shrubs and climbers.

4 One of the most popular foods is black sunflower seed. Fill the special seed feeders to the top as they will soon be emptied. Check occasionally that the outlets haven't become blocked.

 = Watch out! Sharp or dangerous tool in use. = Watch out! Adult help is needed.

7 Store food in a cool, dry place, protected from mice, and always wash your hands after dealing with the food and the feeders. Clean away debris beneath hanging feeders and bird tables.

5 Peanuts are taken by a wide range of birds, especially in winter, and also by squirrels. Use a metal holder with an outer mesh guard to prevent squirrels gnawing through.

6 A good bird feeder will come apart for cleaning and the removal of stale food. This is very important with peanut feeders as mouldy peanuts are toxic. A swivel hanger deters squirrels.

8 Though it is often recommended that you feed only in winter, there are times when birds can't find enough wild food. Provide a variety of foods and plenty of clean water.

TOP TIPS

▶ Always throw away old food before refilling and regularly clean feeders with brushes and mild detergent.
▶ Wash your hands after handling feeders.

Bird feast

Berries are a great natural food for several bird species. This feeding and watering station includes berries plus extra types of food for birds that don't eat berries, and the shrubs will eventually grow to form cover for roosting and nesting.

you will need
- **shrubs** and **plants** (*see* Plant List)
- **bucket** of **water**
- **border fork**
- **border spade**
- **trowel**
- **shallow dish** or **bowl**
- **watering can**
- **bird feeder hangers**
- **bird feeders**
- **fat snacks**
- **peanuts**
- **spike** or **cane (stake)** (optional)
- **chipped bark** (optional)

plant list
- ✳ **1 barberry**
  Berberis thunbergii f. *atropurpurea*
- ✳ **1 cotoneaster**
  Cotoneaster conspicuus 'Decorus'
- ✳ **1 firethorn**
  Pyracantha 'Golden Charmer'
- ✳ **1 laurustinus**
  Viburnum tinus
- ✳ **1 pheasant berry**
  Leycesteria formosa 'Golden Lanterns'
- ✳ **5 thymes**
  Thymus 'Doone Valley'

FACT FILE
COTONEASTER KNOW-HOW
This shrub is best known for its crops of ornamental berries, which are gorged on by local garden birds as well as visiting migrants. Cotoneasters are also good bee and hoverfly plants, bearing hundreds of nectar-rich blooms.

cotoneaster

WARNING – Many berries are poisonous to humans.

1 Plunge all the plants in a bucket of water and wait for the bubbles to stop. Fork over the ground to break up any lumps. You may need adult help. Remove all visible weeds and weed roots. Set out the plants.

2 Place the tall firethorn about 45cm/18in from the fence and angle the top of the plant in towards it. If you plant too close, it may not get enough water. Arrange the rest of the plants according to height.

(!) 3 Dig a hole for the cotoneaster. The plant shown here is potbound. If you see this, gently loosen a few of the roots to encourage them to spread once planted.

4 Replace the soil using a trowel, firming in around the root-ball with your hands. Repeat for all the other shrubs. Next, set a shallow dish or bowl into the ground.

5 Plant the creeping thyme plants around the birdbath to cover the bare ground. These plants will attract bees, which will also pollinate the berrying shrubs. Water all the plants.

6 Push hanging bird feeder supports into the soil and attach two types of feeder – the one shaped like an apple contains peanuts and the other is designed for fat snacks.

7 Pour water into the birdbath. This shallow dish is ideal for birds to drink from and bathe in and will be easy to clean out frequently. Use a soft hand brush and watering can for cleaning.

8 If you have some windfall apples, push a few on to a long spike or cane for the birds to peck at and enjoy. Ask an adult to help you, as the cores can be quite hard.

TOP TIP
▶ To keep down weeds after planting this permanent shrub border, cover the ground with a mulch of chipped bark to 5–8cm/2–3in deep.

bird feast

Create a wild lawn

If a weed-infested lawn is left to grow long, you'll find all kinds of flowers coming into bloom – a treat for bees and hoverflies. Try adding some bulbs and other wild flowers.

you will need
- **long-handled bulb planter**
- **low-growing spring bulbs** (*see* Plant List), 1–2 bags
- **trowel**
- **lawn 'weeds'** or **wildflower 'plugs'** (*see* Plant List)

plant list
bulbs
- ✳ **Crocus**
  Crocus tommasinianus
- ✳ **Grape hyacinth**
  Muscari armeniacum
- ✳ **Snake's head fritillary**
  Fritillaria meleagris

wild flowers
- ✳ **Autumn hawkbit, fall dandelion**
  Leontodon autumnalis

- ✳ **Bird's-foot trefoil**
  Lotus corniculatus
- ✳ **Common daisy**
  Bellis perennis
- ✳ **Oxeye daisy**
  Leucanthemum vulgare
- ✳ **Ribwort (narrowleaf) plantain**
  Plantago lanceolata
- ✳ **Self heal**
  Prunella vulgaris
- ✳ **Yarrow**
  Achillea millefolium

1 Check the bulb packet for the planting depth and take out circles of turf to the right depth using a long-handled bulb planter.

2 You may need an adult to help you make more holes. Choose an area where grass can be longer.

3 Plant one or two bulbs in each hole. You could alternate which type of bulb you put in the holes so you create a mixed flower effect.

4 Repeat until you have planted bulbs in each of the holes.

5 Replace the turf plugs as you go and firm in with your foot.

6 To plant extra wildflower plugs or young, pot-grown plants, dig out a chunk of turf with a trowel or bulb planter and press the plant firmly into the space.

TOP TIP
► To encourage more wildflowers, don't use any kind of fertilizer. Mow the lawn in autumn and after the bulbs have died down in spring and a few times in summer. Let the plants drop seed.

 = Watch out! Sharp or dangerous tool in use. = Watch out! Adult help is needed.

Grow a wildlife hedge

Plant a hedge with native shrubs and trees that have nectar-rich flowers, berries, fruits and nuts. This will feed the wildlife and offer safe roosting and nesting spots.

you will need

- border spade
- border fork
- well-rotted garden compost or manure
- slow-release fertilizer granules

chipped bark

- mixed bare-rooted country or **wild hedging shrubs** or **trees** (*see* Plant List)
- **bucket** of water
- **measured stick** or **cane**
- **secateurs** or **pruners**
- **watering can**
- **chipped bark**

plant list

- ✳ **Blackthorn/sloe**
  Prunus spinosa
- ✳ **Dog rose**
  Rosa canina
- ✳ **Elder, black elderberry**
  Sambucus nigra
- ✳ **Field (hedge) maple**

Acer campestre
- ✳ **Hawthorn**
  Crataegus monogyna
- ✳ **Hazel**
  Corylus avellana

WARNING – Some native hedge plants are poisonous if eaten.

1 Ask an adult to help you dig a trench to a spade's depth. Fork in well-rotted compost or manure.

2 Sprinkle slow-release fertilizer granules on to the soil following packet instructions. This will mix in when you replace the soil.

3 Half an hour before planting, remove the outer wrapping protecting the hedge roots and soak in a bucket of water.

4 Mark a stick or cane with the correct planting distance (about 25–30cm/10–12in).

5 Use this to space the plants in the trench.

6 Trim overlong roots with secateurs (adult supervision is required) and spread them out. Holding the stem upright, work soil back around the roots. This is a two-person job.

7 Plant the hedging plants at the same depth as they were originally planted – you will see a dark stain on the stems.

8 Firm in lightly with your foot and water. Mulch with chipped bark to prevent weeds growing.

Make a mini meadow

It's easy to create your own patch of meadow in the garden. All you have to do is prepare an area of earth and sow annual flower seeds, which look pretty and also attract insects. Try to use plants that grow wild near where you live, as insects will like these best.

you will need
- **border fork**
- **soil rake**
- **hardy annual seed**
  (see Plant List)
- **sand** (optional)
- **stick** (optional)
- **watering can**

corn marigold   *field poppy*   *annual mallow*

plant list
* **Annual mallow**
  Lavatera trimestris
* **Californian poppy**
  Eschscholzia californica
* **Corn chamomile, Roman chamomile**
  Chamaemelum nobile
* **Cornflower**
  Centaurea cyanus
* **Corn marigold, corn daisy**
  Chrysanthemum segetum
* **Field poppy, corn poppy**
  Papaver rhoeas
* **Love-in-a-mist, devil in the bush**
  Nigella damascena
* **Meadow cranesbill**
  Geranium pratense
* **Nasturtium**
  Tropaeolum majus
* **Pot marigold**

FACT FILE
CORNFLOWERS
Before wheat or corn seed could be purified, and before the introduction of weedkillers, cornfield annuals were a familiar sight, benefiting many different creatures. Some farmers are now beginning to re-introduce the flowers into their fields to great benefit. It is known that they secrete a root substance that actually helps wheat to grow.

cornflower

1 Fork over the ground to loosen the soil and break up large any large clods. Remove all visible weeds and weed out roots. Rake level and work the soil to create a fine crumb-like surface. Adult supervision is required.

2 Buy a mixture of cornfield flower seeds or make up your own mix combining plants from the Plant List. You can also add hardy annuals to perennial flower borders to increase nectar levels.

3 The traditional way of sowing cornfields was to scatter the seed by hand in a wide sweeping motion called 'broadcasting'. To see where you've been and to sow the seed more evenly, consider mixing it with sand.

4 An alternative to broadcasting your seed is to mark out patches in the soil using a stick and sowing just one variety in each patch. This still gives a natural look but the colours are solid blocks rather than all mixed up.

5 Many hardy annuals need light before they germinate so be careful not to bury the seed with soil as you walk about sowing it in areas that have not yet been sown.

 = Watch out! Sharp or dangerous tool in use.   = Watch out! Adult help is needed.

7 Water the area with a watering can if the weather is particularly dry and sunny and repeat later if the young plants appear to be struggling with drought. Keep on top of weeds, removing them as soon as you see them.

9 You could also sow perennial wildflower mixtures for a permanent meadow that includes plants that tolerate less vigorous grasses, such as meadow cranesbill and the lesser knapweed (illustrated).

6 Once you have sown all the seed, lightly rake over the whole area and, to bring the seed in close contact with the soil, gently press down the earth with the flat side of the head of the rake.

8 To get cornfield annuals to flower the following year, in spring, the old meadow must be forked over. This triggers germination. Sprinkle extra seed to guarantee displays.

TOP TIP

▶ You can sow cornfield annuals in large wooden barrels, plastic tubs and large clay or glazed pots. Keep well watered throughout the growing period.

Buzzing blooms

Plant bee-friendly flowers rich in pollen and nectar and you will be helping these creatures to thrive. In addition, the more bees that visit your garden and pollinate your flowers, the bigger your crops of fruit and vegetables will be! Bees are especially attracted to single rather than double blooms, in blue and purple, white and yellow. They can even see flower shapes and patterns that show up in ultraviolet light, which are invisible to humans.

you will need
- **border spade**
- **grit** (optional)
- **perennials** (see Plant List)
- **bucket** of **water**
- **bamboo cane** (stick)
- **border fork**
- **watering can** with a **fine rose** (sprinkler head) attachment

pincushion flower

purple top verbena

plant list

S= small; M=medium; T= tall

✳ **Bee balm**
Monarda didyma M–T

✳ **Bidens, Apache beggarsticks**
Bidens ferulifolia S

✳ **Borage/starflower**
Borago officinalis M

✳ **Catmint/catnip**
Nepeta 'Six Hills Giant' M–T

✳ **Cosmos, Mexican aster**
Cosmos bippinatus T

✳ **Cranesbill**
Geranium 'Johnson's Blue' M

✳ **Fiddleneck, lacy phacelia**
Phacelia tanacetifolia S–M

✳ **Hollyhock**
Alcea rosea T

✳ **Jacob's ladder**
Polemonium caeruleum M–T

✳ **Lavender**
Lavandula angustifolia 'Munstead' M

✳ **Lupin**
Lupinus (blue/purple spp./hybrids) T

✳ **Penstemon, beardtongue**
Penstemon (pink flowered cvs.) M–T

✳ **Pincushion flower**
Scabiosa atropurpurea 'Chile Black' M

✳ **Pink hyssop**
Agastache barberi M

✳ **Purple top verbena**
Verbena bonariensis T

✳ **Rosemary**
Rosmarinus officinalis T

✳ **Sage (ornamental and culinary types)**
Salvia spp./cvs. M–T

✳ **Snowdrop**
Galanthus spp./cvs. S

✳ **Squill**
Scilla spp./cvs. S

✳ **Sunflower**
Helianthus annuus T

✳ **Thyme**
Thymus spp./cvs. S

 1 Choose a sunny spot and turn over the soil, breaking up clods. If necessary, work in grit to improve drainage. Ask an adult to help. Plunge the plants in a bucket of water and wait for the bubbles to stop.

2 Plant the border in sections so that you have room to work. Lay out the plants with the lower growing ones towards the front and taller plants towards the back.

 3 Once you are happy with the position of all of the plants, dig the first planting hole with a spade, making it wider than the pot, but the same depth as the height of the pot.

4 Try the pot for size in the hole. It shouldn't be too shallow, as this will make the plant vulnerable to drying out, or too deep, as this can cause rotting. Adjust as necessary.

 = Watch out! Sharp or dangerous tool in use. = Watch out! Adult help is needed.

FACT FILE

HONEY VERSUS BUMBLE

Bumble-bees are among the first insects to appear in late winter and survive on early spring flowers, such as bulbs, alpines and wild plants. It is not warm enough for honey bees until later in spring. Bumble-bees are large, rounded and furry and honey bees are elongated, with smooth bodies. Only honey bees make honey.

honey bee

bumble-bee

5 Carefully take the plant out of its pot. You might struggle if the plant is very well rooted. Tap the base sharply on a hard surface to loosen or ask an adult to help.

6 Plant, then check that the top surface of the root-ball is at the same level as the surrounding soil – lay a cane across the hole to check, if you like. Backfill with loose soil.

7 Firm the soil with your hands, checking that you have filled all the gaps. Continue planting all the plants, then level the surrounding soil using a border fork.

8 Water the plants in thoroughly. To extend the border, follow the same method, perhaps repeating blocks or swathes of the same varieties, or introduce different plants.

Hoverfly hotel

These pots of citrus-coloured blooms will be a magnet for hoverflies. Often mistaken for wasps or honey bees, hoverflies are completely harmless. You'll find them visiting many of the same flowers as bees and butterflies but they especially like yellow, orange and white blooms, daisies and heads made up of many tiny flowers.

you will need

- **assorted plants** (*see* Plant List, we used pot marigolds and tickseed plants)
- **bucket** of **water**
- **polystyrene (Styrofoam) pieces**
- **blue glazed pots**, 2
- **gravel**
- **trowel**
- **peat free-potting compost** with **added loam (soil mix)**
- **watering can**
- **liquid plant food**

plant list

- ❋ **Black-eyed Susan**
  Rudbeckia fulgida
- ❋ **Common daisy**
  Bellis perennis
- ❋ **Fennel**
  Foeniculum vulgare
- ❋ **Feverfew**
  Chrysanthemum parthenium
- ❋ **Masterwort**
  Astrantia major

- ❋ **Milfoil, yarrow**
  Achillea 'Moonshine'
- ❋ **Pot marigold**
  Calendula officinalis
- ❋ **Poached egg plant, Douglas' meadowfarm**
  Limnanthes douglasii
- ❋ **Stonecrop**
  Sedum spurium

- ❋ **Sunflower**
  Helianthus annuus
- ❋ **Sweet alyssum**
  Lobularia maritima
- ❋ **Tagetes**
  Tagetes tenuifolia 'Lemon Gem'
- ❋ **Tickseed**
  Coreopsis grandiflora 'Early Sunrise'

FACT FILE

GARDENER'S FRIEND

Adult hoverflies pollinate flowers just like bees and their eggs hatch into larvae, which eat huge numbers of greenfly or aphids as well as other common garden pests. Luring adult hoverflies into the garden with their favourite blooms is an easy and natural way of reducing problems on plants such as roses.

adult hoverfly

1 Plunge the plants in a bucket of water and wait for the bubbles to stop. Place broken-up chunks of polystyrene in the bottom of one pot. Add a couple of handfuls of gravel.

2 Cover with compost, nearly filling the pot but allowing space for the root-balls. Ease the young plants out of their tray, pushing your thumb through the drainage holes.

3 Choose young, vigorous plants with a few unopened flower-buds and a good root system. Avoid pot-bound plants. Space the plants out and fill the gaps in between with compost.

4 Prepare a second container, following the same method as before. Add a small amount of compost and try plants of tickseed (*Coreopsis*) for size. Remove from their pots.

 = Watch out! Sharp or dangerous tool in use. 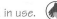 = Watch out! Adult help is needed.

8 Both the pot marigolds and the tickseeds will only keep flowering if you pinch off the fading flowers regularly and prevent them from setting seed. Water regularly and feed every two weeks.

5 Place the first plant in the pot. The top of the root-ball should be about 2.5cm (1in) below the top of the pot. Add or remove more compost to adjust the level if necessary.

6 Add a few more plants, spacing them equally. If you like, you could also grow these plants from seed, sowing them in early spring on a warm windowsill.

7 Finish planting, carefully working more compost into the gaps between the root-balls. Lift the leaves, taking care not to bury them. Firm with your fingers and water.

pot marigold

Log garden

This little fernery makes an interesting feature for a shady wild corner and will make a cosy home for all kinds of minibeasts, such as insects, amphibians and small mammals. Ideally it should be kept moist, so water if it gets dry.

you will need
- **logs** and/or **tree branches**
- **wedges** of **wood**
- **fern selection** (see Plant List)
- **bucket** of **water**
- **peat free-potting compost** with **added loam (soil mix)**
- **leaf mould**, home-made (optional)
- **trowel**
- **bark pieces** or **chippings**
- **twisted branches** or **roots**, **driftwood**, or **pine cones**

plant list
- **Common polypody** *Polypodium vulgare*
- **Copper shield fern, Japanese autumn fern** *Dryopteris erythrosora*
- **Hard shield fern** *Polystichum aculeatum*
- **Japanese painted fern** *Athyrium niponicum var. pictum*
- **Scaly male fern** *Dryopteris affinis*
- **Soft shield fern** *Polystichum setiferum* Divisilobum Group

FACT FILE
DINOSAUR PLANTS
Ferns go back 360 million years and would have been the main ground-cover plant when dinosaurs roamed the earth! They reproduce via spores, usually produced in clusters on the back of their fronds – have a look! The spores are so tiny that they float round the world on air.

fern frond

1 Lay out a series of long logs or tree branches in a shady spot. Raise them up with wedges of wood to create planting pockets. You may need adult help. Soak the ferns in a bucket of water.

2 Fill the gaps between the logs with compost. Ferns don't need any extra fertilizer, but you could add some home-made leaf mould to make the soil more like that of a woodland.

3 Lay out all the ferns, working out which combination of leaf form and texture looks best. Take the soft shield fern out of its pot giving the base a tap on a hard surface if it sticks.

4 Dig a hole in the compost with a trowel and put the fern in it. Fill around the roots with compost and firm gently with your hands. Take care not to bury any fronds.

5 The soft shield fern and the copper shield fern are both evergreen, so the leaves will remain attractive all through the winter. The copper shield fern's fronds are pinky-orange when young.

6 For decoration and to fill gaps between the ferns, remove pieces of bark from logs using a trowel. The best way to do this is to turn the trowel upside down, wedge it under a loose corner, then lift.

(!) = Watch out! Sharp or dangerous tool in use. = Watch out! Adult help is needed.

7 Work the bark that you have collected in around the plants. If you don't have enough, use decorative chipped bark mulch. This will help to keep down weeds and retain moisture.

8 Look out for pine cones, interestingly shaped pieces of branch or root (even driftwood from the beach) and use them to add the finishing touch to your 'fernery'.

lizard

FACT FILE
DINO GARDEN
Lizards are descended from dinosaurs and many can lose their tails to escape a predator, then regrow a new one.

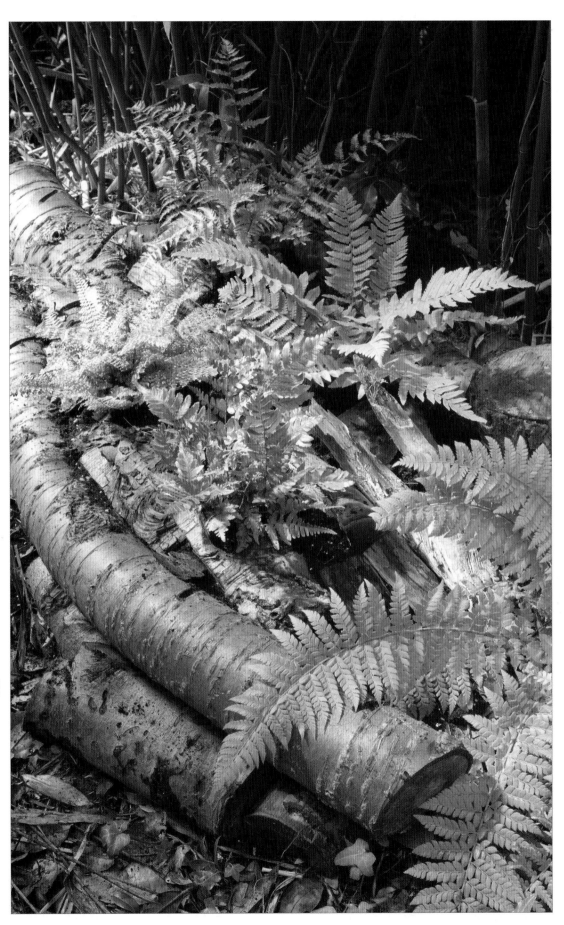

Mini wildlife pond

This pond will be a wildlife magnet and in spring and summer you'll have some great backyard safari moments as frogs dive for cover and birds line up for a bath. Position it next to some long grass or evergreen plants so that creatures have somewhere to hide. You must ask adult permission before making this pond, and it is not suitable if there are very young children around.

you will need
- spade
- **large black plastic container** (around 30 x 65cm/12 x 26in)
- **gravel**
- **straight piece of wood**
- **spirit (carpenter's) level**
- **house bricks**
- **large cobbles**
- **small cobbles** and **pebbles**
- **small pieces of turf**
- **marginal plants** (see Plant List), soaked in a bucket of water

plant list
❋ **Marsh pennywort**
   Hydrocotyle vulgaris
❋ **Miniature bulrush/dwarf reedmace**
   Typha minima

Warning!
Ponds or water features are not recommended in gardens with children under the age of six as they can drown in even very shallow water. Children should never be around water of any type or depth without adult supervision at all times.

FACT FILE
POND VISITORS
A tiny pond such as this can attract a surprising number of animals. Insects will fly in for a drink, a frog or two will soon take up residence and the glint of water will also attract dragonflies on the look out for their next meal. Birds not only drink but also bathe, standing on the pebbles. And at night, depending on where you live, hedgehogs and other nocturnal creatures will call by.

green dragonfly

1 Using a spade, dig a hole just large enough to slot the container into. The reservoir tanks you can buy for self-contained water features are ideal for creating mini ponds. Adult supervision is required.

2 Try the container for size. The base should rest evenly on the soil at the bottom of the hole so that it is properly supported. The rim should be level with or just below the soil. You may need adult help.

3 To create the pond floor and encourage aquatic or water-dwelling creatures to inhabit it, fill the base of the container with washed gravel to a depth of about 5cm/2in. Ask an adult to help you.

4 Check that the pond is level by placing a piece of wood across and resting a spirit level on it. The moving bubble should be right in the middle. Next build a simple stack of bricks in the container.

 = Watch out! Sharp or dangerous tool in use.   = Watch out! Adult help is needed.

5 Check the bricks are secure, then top them with one large cobble. Add smaller cobbles and pebbles to camouflage the bricks and create a ramp for easy access. Fill the pond with water.

6 The cobbles allow creatures to get safely into the water and if they fall in, to help them scramble out again. Blend the container edge in by covering it with some large and small cobbles.

7 If the pond is next to a lawn, squeeze in some small pieces of turf and low-growing weeds or wild plants to create easy access to the water and camouflage the hard rim of the container.

8 Create platforms with submerged bricks for the marginal (pond edge) plants to sit on. The surface of the pots should be just below the water. Fence off the pond so young children cannot go near it.

Plant profiles

The following pages describe how to grow and use many of the plants included in previous chapters, so you can check where they like to live and how they like to be treated. There are sections on growing for colour and scent, plants for pots and containers, and lots of plants you can eat, including vegetables, herbs and fruits – yummy!

Planting for colour

Crocus
Crocus chrysanthus
Flowering in late winter and early spring, these colourful little bulbs are very cheering. Plant in groups at the front of the border, along the edges of pathways, in a rock garden or alpine troughs, or in bowls on the patio. Varieties include 'Blue Pearl', 'Zwanenburg Bronze' and the two-tone 'Ladykiller'.
How to grow Plant in late summer or early autumn, 5–7.5cm/2–3in deep in well-drained soil and full sun. Cut lawns six weeks after flowering.
Height and spread 7.5–10 x 5–7.5cm/3–4 x 2–3in.
Hardiness ✽✽✽ Zone 3.
Other plants Dutch crocus (C. vernus forms) flower slightly later and have larger blooms. 'Jeanne d'Arc' (white), 'Pickwick' (purple-and-white striped) and 'Remembrance' (purple) are good in pots and borders or naturalized in lawns (see page 107). Also plant the early C. x luteus 'Golden Yellow' in lawns.

Dahlia
Dahlia cultivars
Vibrant late summer- and autumn-flowering plants, these have large blooms in various shapes and forms. They include pompon, cactus, water lily, collerette and decorative types in reds, oranges, yellows, pinks, purples and white. Some are dazzling two-tone cultivars and many have purple-black leaves. They are perfect for large patio pots or filling border gaps.
How to grow Start tubers into growth in early spring (see page 91). Move outdoors from early summer, after hardening off in well-drained but moisture-retentive soil. Protect from slugs. Deadhead regularly and feed generously when in flower. May need staking or support. In colder areas, lift tubers in mid-autumn, storing in a frost-free place. Otherwise, mulch well to protect from the cold.
Height and spread 60–120 x 45–60cm/24–48 x 18–24in.
Hardiness ✽ Zone 8.
Other plants Single dahlias, such as the Coltness hybrids, are good for bees and butterflies. These, and the dwarf bedding and patio types, are grown from seed.

Hollyhock
Alcea rosea
These cottage garden plants have tall spires of single or double blooms in midsummer, which take up little room. There are many shades, from dark reds to pastels. Leaves have rounded lobes. Short-lived perennials, they are usually grown as biennials (meaning they flower the second year from sowing) or annuals. Use tall varieties to give height in borders or to frame a doorway.
How to grow Sow seed in pots or trays on a windowsill in early spring (for annuals), or outdoors, in an unheated greenhouse or cold frame in early summer (for biennials). With annuals, prick out into individual pots to grow on before planting. Alternatively, buy young plants in spring. They require full sun and well-drained soil. Discard after flowering to reduce the chance of hollyhock rust disease.
Height and spread 100–200cm x 30–40cm/40–80 x 12–16in.
Hardiness ✽✽✽ Zone 3
Other plants Majorette Group, which are compact annuals with double or semi-double blooms. The tall annuals, Summer Carnival Group. Chater's Double Group, which are tall and usually grown as biennials. The nearly black A. rosea 'Nigra' is very dramatic and unusual.

Mexican aster
Cosmos bipinnatus Sonata Series
This half-hardy annual produces lots of big, dish-shaped blooms in shades of pink and white all summer long. The slender stems carry frothy, divided leaves. It is great for borders.
How to grow Sow seed in pots or trays of seed compost on a warm windowsill in early spring. Prick out seedlings and grow on in good light. Harden off and plant out after the last likely frost for your area. It will grow in any well-drained soil, even if it is relatively poor, in full sun. Deadhead regularly. May need staking/support.
Height and spread 60 x 38cm/24 x 15in.
Hardiness ✽ Zone 7.
Other plants 'Purity' is, as its name suggests, a white form.

Ornamental onion
Allium 'Purple Sensation'
The drumstick heads of this onion family member open as the spring bulbs start to fade and early summer flowering herbaceous perennials are coming into bloom. Their vivid colour stands out well and they add height while other plants are still quite low.

▲ Spring-flowering crocus

▲ Dahlia

▲ Hollyhock

▲ Mexican aster

▲ *Ornamental onion*

▲ *Beard tongue*

▲ *Red hot poker*

▲ *Snapdragon*

How to grow Plant the pale round bulbs in autumn, 13cm/5in deep, putting three to a 25cm/10in pot. Stand in a sheltered spot outdoors but don't allow them to dry out. Alternatively, plant in groups of three or five direct in the border. In spring, when the thin green leaves appear, plant potted bulbs in gaps in the border. Leaves die before flowers open. They require full sun to light shade and any well-drained soil.
Height and spread 100 x 7.5cm/40 x 3in.
Hardiness ✳✳✳ Zone 4.
Other plants For even bigger drumsticks on tall stems try *A*. 'Globemaster'. For big, starry heads on short stems, grow *A. christophii* or even more starry, *A. schubertii*.

Beard tongue
Penstemon
Flowering from midsummer to mid-autumn, these perennials are great value. Blooms are tubular with flared ends and often streaked inside with darker or lighter markings. Colours range from deep burgundy or purple through shades of red and pink to white. Narrow-leaved forms such as 'Schoenholzeri' (syn. 'Firebird') are generally hardier than broad-leaved ones. Best in a border with circular or daisy shaped blooms.

How to grow Grow in full sun in any well-drained soil. They are easy to propagate from shoot tip cuttings in summer. Best planted in late spring/early summer in cold areas. Deadhead flower spikes before they have finished flowering completely to encourage more spikes. Leave late seed-heads on for extra frost protection. Cut back to a low framework of branches in mid-spring, just above where new growth is sprouting.
Height and spread 60–90 x 30–60cm/24–36 x 12–24in.
Hardiness ✳✳✳ Zones 6–9
Other plants For front of border positions try the pink 'Evelyn'. Bird Series include the pink and white 'Osprey' and dark purple 'Blackbird'. There are many more, including the pale pink 'Apple Blossom' and soft purple 'Stapleford Gem'.

Red hot poker
Kniphofia
These bold, late summer- to early autumn-flowering perennials from South Africa are also known as torch lilies. This is because of the shape of the flowers and the orange-turning-to-yellow colouring of many species and cultivars. Dainty, single-coloured pokers are also available. Foliage is grassy to sword-shaped and some are virtually evergreen. Good for adding an exotic feel.

How to grow They require full sun in well-drained, moisture-retentive soil, so add manure or compost to dry soils. Apply a dry mulch of bark or pine needles in autumn to protect the crowns in cold regions. Cut off old spikes at the base and tidy foliage in spring.
Height and spread 60–150 x 45–60+cm/24–60 x 18–24+in.
Hardiness ✳✳ Zone 5.
Other plants 'Samuel's Sensation' is a classic red hot poker. 'Alcazar' has vivid orange spikes and 'Percy's Pride' is greenish yellow.

Snapdragon
Antirrhinum majus
These plants are grown as half-hardy bedding specimens. Taller types are great for filling gaps in borders. You can make the flower 'mouths' open and close by squeezing, hence the name snapdragon.
How to grow They are easy to grow from seed on a warm windowsill in spring. Pinch out the tips of young plants to promote branching and more flowers. Plant out in late spring, after they have been hardened off, in any fertile, well-drained soil. Cut off the main flower spike above the lower side shoots when it has faded to encourage more spikes.
Height and spread 60–75 x 30–45cm/24–30 x 12–18in.
Hardiness ✳✳ Zone 7.

Other plants Coronette Series is resistant to the fungal disease rust, while Sonnet Series does well in rainy summers. Madame Butterfly Series has tall stems and double flowers and 'Magic Carpet' is a compact bedding or patio pot type.

Other colourful plants
* **Blanket flower** (yellow/orange/red) *Gaillardia* x *grandiflora*
* **Coneflower** (gold/orange/red) *Rudbeckia hirta* 'Marmalade'
* **Day lily** (yellow) *Hemerocallis* 'Stella de Oro'
* **Fuchsia** (pink/purple/red/white) *Fuchsia* cvs.
* **Gladioli** (pink/purple/orange/red/white) *Gladiolus* cvs.
* **Montbretia** (red) *Crocosmia* 'Lucifer'
* **Ornamental sage** (purple) *Salvia* x *superba*
* **Osteospermum** (pink) *Osteospermum* Sunny Series
* **Spider flower** (white/pink/mauve) *Cleome hassleriana*
* **Tree mallow** (pink) *Lavatera* x *clementii* cvs.

Planting for scent

Candytuft
Iberis umbellata

This quick and easy hardy annual flower (a member of the mustard family) is grown for its pretty pastel blooms and for its sweet fragrance. This is especially good in white and long-established seed mixtures. It attracts butterflies.

How to grow Rake an area of soil until it looks like fine breadcrumbs. Sow thinly, lightly covering the seed with soil. Repeat between early spring and midsummer for a succession of blooms around the garden or in pots.

Height and spread 15–30 x 15–30cm/6–12 x 6–12in.

Hardiness ❋❋❋ Zone 3.

Other plants For colour mixtures try 'Fairy' or 'Fairyland Mixed', 'Fantasia Mixed' and 'Flash', all of which have shallowly domed heads made up of many small blooms. 'Giant Hyacinth Flowered' is white with the best perfume.

Cherry pie, Heliotrope
Heliotropium arborescens

Although old-fashioned, tender perennial cultivars of *H. arborescens* have the richest perfume, seed-raised plants in a border or pots by the patio will fill the air with their sweet, spicy, vanilla scent. The deep-purple domed heads are shown off by the dark green, crinkled, glossy leaves. It is a good butterfly and moth plant.

How to grow Sow half-hardy annual seed on a warm windowsill or in a heated propagator in spring and prick out seedlings when large enough to handle into individual pots. Harden off before planting out after risk of frost has passed.

Height and spread 45 x 45cm/ 18 x 18in.

Hardiness ❋ Zone 10.

Other plants 'Marine' and the newer 'Nagano' are the main seed varieties, but 'Dwarf Marine' is a compact alternative for baskets.

Daffodil
Narcissus

If you have ever grown 'Paper White' daffodils for indoor flowering, you will know how powerfully fragrant some cultivars are. Outside, in sheltered corners of the patio or around doorways, pots and tubs of fragrant daffodils are a treat in early and mid-spring.

How to grow Plant bulbs three times deeper than the size of the bulb in late summer or autumn but preferably as soon as bulbs are available. Discard any soft or very mouldy bulbs. Any good potting compost (especially loam/soil based ones) will do for containers. Avoid very dry soils. Jonquils appreciate a bed in full sun but most tolerate some shade. Deadhead after flowering and feed with tomato food at the same time to build up bulb reserves for next year. For the same reason, don't knot or cut off the leaves until at least 8 weeks after flowering.

Height and spread 15–45 x 7.5–15cm/6–18 x 3–6in.

Hardiness ❋❋❋ Zone 3.

Other plants Try the large, frilly, double-headed Narcissus 'Cheerfulness' and 'Sir Winston Churchill'. 'Sweetness' has small, deep yellow flowers and the variety 'Actaea' and *N. poeticus* var. *recurvus*, known as pheasant's eye daffodils, are creamy white with an orange 'eye'. Jonquils (*N. jonquilla*) have very dainty yellow flowers and grassy leaves.

Hyacinth
Hyacinthus orientalis

These intensely fragrant flowers can either be grown from 'prepared' bulbs designed for indoor flowering as early as Christmas, or from ordinary bulbs. The stocky flower heads, tightly packed with individual blooms, are held on short flower stems. Flowers last well in patio pots given a little shelter from wind and rain, but bulbs can also be planted with spring bedding in borders.

How to grow Plant in full sun or partial shade. For containers, choose a loam-based potting compost and ensure there is good drainage. Deadhead after flowering, feed with liquid fertilizer and leave foliage to die down to allow bulbs to build up reserves for next year's flowering.

Height and spread 20–25 x 15cm/8–10 x 6in.

Hardiness ❋❋❋ Zone 4.

Other plants For rich blues (which hide fading flowers well) choose cultivars such as 'Delft Blue' and 'Blue Jacket'. 'L'Innocence' is pure white, 'Pink Pearl' mid pink, and 'City of Haarlem' delicate yellow. 'Gypsy Queen' is pale salmon.

Night scented stock
Matthiola longipetala subsp. *bicornis*

Unlike the other types of stock, which are also scented, you grow this hardy annual species for its fragrance rather than for

▲ *Candytuft*

▲ *Cherry pie*

▲ *Daffodil*

▲ *Hyacinth*

▲ *Night scented stock*

▲ *Sweet alyssum*

▲ *Sweet pea*

▲ *Wallflower*

its amazing blooms. Sow in beds under windows or around doors or sprinkle seed in window boxes.

How to grow It prefers a sunny position in well-drained and preferably alkaline soil. Sow seed thinly in spring on to raked soil and cover lightly.
Height and spread 15–30 x 20cm/6–12 x 8in.
Hardiness ✻✻✻ Zone 5.
Other plants Brompton stocks (*M. incana* 'Brompton Mixed') are showy biennials with double blooms in pastel shades. You can buy ready grown plants in spring for flowering in summer. Ten week stocks (*M. incana* 'Ten Week Mixed') are annuals, also with double blooms, which are sown on a windowsill in early spring.

Sweet alyssum
Lobularia maritima
This hardy annual is usually white-flowered. It is often used in hanging baskets and patio beds. The tiny four-petalled blooms are massed in shallow domed heads and the sweet scent attracts lots of insects.
How to grow Sowing directly into a well-raked seedbed in spring is easiest, but you can also grow in seed trays and pots on the windowsill for planting out after hardening off. It prefers well-drained ground but tends to stop flowering and produce seed

if it runs short of water. Deadhead by clipping over with small scissors.
Height and spread 10–20 x 20–30cm/4–8 x 8–12in.
Hardiness ✻✻✻ Zone 3.
Other plants 'Snow Crystals' is longer-flowered than most, making neat domes. 'Sweet White' is strongly scented. Pinks and mauves include Easter Bonnet Series and 'Oriental Night'.

Sweet pea
Lathyrus odoratus
Cultivated modern versions of these hardy annual climbing plants were bred more as a colourful cut flower than for their scent. However, old-fashioned seed mixtures have a stronger scent, and are usually smaller-flowered and in darker or more muted shades.
How to grow Sow in autumn or spring in long, tubular pots (*see* page 92) or into the ground. Plant out pot-raised plants in a sunny spot after hardening off. Prepare the ground, adding lots of manure or garden compost into the bottom of the planting trench. Provide support. Or, plant in tubs containing loam-based potting compost (soil mix) and make a wigwam to fit. Pick flowers often to keep them producing.
Height and spread 120–180 x 30cm/45–70 x 12in.
Hardiness ✻✻✻ Zone 3.

Other plants Varieties labelled as heritage, old-fashioned, antique or heirloom often have excellent fragrance. As well as mixtures, try the historic pink and white 'Painted Lady'.

Wallflower
Erysimum cheiri
These short-lived perennial evergreen plants flower around the same time as tulips and forget-me-nots. The fragrance not only attracts humans but also early butterflies and bees! The four-petalled flowers are often in soft 'tapestry' or old velvet colours. Taller kinds are useful for filling gaps in borders. Compact varieties do well in window boxes and tubs with dwarf bulbs.
How to grow Wallflowers are members of the cabbage family and can suffer from club root disease. However, well-drained alkaline soil will help control the problem. Buy strong-looking plants in autumn and plant firmly. You can raise your own plants from seed in an outdoor seedbed in late spring or early summer. Grow plants on and move to final flowering positions in autumn to overwinter before spring flowering. Discard plants after flowering.
Height and spread 30–45 x 30–45cm/12–18 x 12–18in.
Hardiness ✻✻ Zone 5.
Other plants Grow the

compact Bedder Series, 'Harlequin' and 'Persian Carpet' in pots, troughs or front of border. 'Cloth of Gold' is a taller, single yellow variety.

Other scented plants
* **Chamomile** (creeping) *Chamaemelum nobile* 'Treneague'
* **Clove scented pinks** *Dianthus* cvs.
* **Curry plant** *Helichrysum italicum*
* **Honeysuckle** (Late Dutch) *Lonicera periclymenum* 'Serotina'
* **Jasmine** *Jasminum officinale*
* **Lavender** *Lavandula angustifolia* cvs.
* **Lemon balm** *Melissa officinalis*
* **Lemon-scented geraniums** *Pelargonium* 'Graveolens'
* **Lily** (scented types) *Lilium* African Queen Group
* **Pansy/viola** *Viola*
* **Sweet William** *Dianthus barbatus*
* **Thyme** (creeping) *Thymus* spp. and cvs.

Planting for pots and containers

Busy Lizzie
Impatiens walleriana
Cheerful busy Lizzies can brighten up any shady corner. They are ideal for patio containers since they flower from the time they are planted out in early summer until the frosts start.

How to grow The fine seed is difficult to handle, so buy plug plants instead and pot them up on a warm windowsill until the weather is warm enough to harden them off. Little deadheading is needed but, after rain, fallen petals stick to the leaves so pick off fading flowers. Red and orange blossoms show rain damage more than pastels, and doubles are less reliable outdoors. Feed and water regularly.

Height and spread 20–30 x 20–30cm/8–12 x 8–12in.

Hardiness ✳ Zone 10.

Other plants F1 hybrid series such as 'Accent' are the best for bedding. Single-coloured, coloured-edged and striped flowers or ones with a contrasting 'eye' are available along with mixtures. For sheltered spots, try New Guinea Hybrids, which have larger flowers in vivid shades and larger, often bronze-tinted or variegated foliage.

French marigold
Tagetes patula
There are many bright varieties of this easy, showy half-hardy annual to choose from. They are often golden yellow or orange, but sometimes deep red or bicoloured (have two colours). They mix well with blue and purple bedding plants. Singles rather than full doubles are better for attracting insects such as hoverflies, but any are useful for discouraging white fly.

How to grow Sow the large seed on a warm windowsill in early spring. Pot on (prick out) seedlings and harden off before planting out after the risk of frost has passed. Look out for slugs. Deadhead frequently.

Height and spread 15–25 x 20–25cm/6–10 x 8–10in.

Hardiness ✳ Zone 9.

Other plants Also try the larger hybrid Afro-French marigolds, such as *Tagetes* 'Zenith Mixed', and the low domes studded with flowers of *Tagetes* 'Lemon Gem'.

Geranium
Pelargonium
If you aren't able to water plants regularly, geraniums, properly called pelargoniums, are great for sun-drenched pots. There are types to suit all kinds of container and colour schemes, with a range from brilliant reds, oranges and cerise-purples to soft lilac, apple blossom-pink and white. Not everyone likes the smell of geranium leaves but you only notice it when you tidy the plants.

How to grow You have to start off plants early if you want to grow them from seed, and seedlings require very good light to thrive. Propagation from cuttings in late summer is a better option, and is an easy way to overwinter plants if you don't have a frost-free greenhouse. Grow in full sun in free-draining, soil-based compost (soil mix). Deadhead regularly, picking off brown petals and seedheads from within the flower cluster. Don't overfeed or overwater.

Height and spread 30–40 x 30–60cm/12–16 x 12–24in.

Hardiness ✳ Zone 9.

Other plants Upright bedding geraniums are usually zonal types, with rounded, hairy leaves with a darker banding. Ivy leaved pelargoniums such as the balcony or cascade types have a trailing habit with wiry stems and small, glossy lobed leaves. The flower clusters may be smaller but there is often more of them.

Petunia
Petunia
There are many types of petunia to choose from, and they come in a lots of colours, including ones with striped, edged or darkly veined flowers. Some have a lovely sweet fragrance after sundown. Bushy, compact forms are ideal where you don't have much space and the trailing kinds work well in baskets. Large, double flowers can suffer in rainy summers.

How to grow Protect from slugs and snails. Starting bedding types from seed is tricky as the seed is very fine and needs light to germinate. Try potting on (pricking out) boxes of seedlings or using little plug plants instead. Plant in pots and baskets after all risk of frost has passed. Grow in a warm, sunny spot. Feed and water regularly and deadhead.

Height and spread 15–30 x 45–120cm/6–12 x 18–48in.

Hardiness ✳ Zone 7.

Other plants For baskets, choose trailing kinds such as Surfinia and Tumbelina Series or, for masses of small cascading blooms, grow the related *Calibrachoa*, such as Million Bells Series. Compact-growing multiflora petunias work well for pots.

▲ *Busy Lizzie*

▲ *French marigold*

▲ *Geranium*

▲ *Petunia*

▲ *Trailing verbena*

▲ *Tulip*

▲ *Tumbling tomato*

▲ *Twin spur*

Trailing verbena
Verbena cvs.
The newer, strong-growing varieties of these tender perennial trailing plants are smothered in blooms all summer. The small flowers are clustered into dome-shaped heads that are very attractive to butterflies and hoverflies and many have a sweet scent. They are now available in most shades, apart from yellow, and plants have neat, toothed-edged or sometimes ferny leaves and wiry spreading or trailing stems.

How to grow Buy trailers as rooted cuttings or young plants in spring and plant up in pots and baskets when all risk of frost has passed. Use any compost (soil mix) recommended for containers and feed and water regularly. Drought and overhead watering can promote powdery mildew disease. Deadhead before flower-heads have completely faded as it can be difficult to tell seed-heads from flower-buds! Take cuttings in late summer and overwinter in a frost-free location.

Height and spread 20–25 x 20–45cm/8–10 x 8–18in.
Hardiness ✳ Zone 7.
Other plants
Tapien, Temari and Babylon Series are all excellent for hanging baskets. Quartz Series plants are bushy and upright, ideal for pots.

Tulip
Tulipa cvs.
Some tulips flower early in spring, but most bloom a bit later and are perfect for bringing colour on to the patio. Tulips come in all colours and some have striped or streaked petals, frills and flounces.

How to grow Plant bulbs in mid- to late autumn in pots using well-draining potting compost (soil mix). Stand the pots in a sheltered spot outside. Don't let the compost dry out. Move to a sunny spot when the shoots appear. To help build up the bulb, deadhead, feed with tomato food and allow leaves to die down naturally.

Height and spread 20–60 x 15cm/8–24 x 6in.
Hardiness ✳✳✳ Zone 3.
Other plants 'Greigii' and 'Kaufmanniana' types are dwarf and early flowering. Some, such as 'Red Riding Hood', have striped leaves. The early double 'Angelique' has full blooms of pale pink, white and green. Later tall, lily flowered tulips such as 'China Pink' make a striking display in a container.

Tumbler tomatoes
Lycopersicon esculentum
Some plants seem made for pots and baskets and this variety is patio perfect.

How to grow These tender plants need warmth to thrive, so you'll need to keep them in a sheltered spot until the risk of frost has passed or move under cover on chilly nights. Choose a moisture-retentive potting compost (soil mix) or add water-retaining gel crystals, especially to hanging baskets. Feed and water regularly, changing to a high-potassium food when flowers appear.

Height and spread 30–60cm/ 12–24in.
Hardiness ✳ Zone N/A.
Other plants As well as 'Tumbler' you could grow 'Gartenperle', 'Hundreds and Thousands' and red or yellow 'Tumbling Tom' varieties. For larger tomatoes, try 'Totem'.

Twin spur
Diascia
This tender perennial produces a froth of shell-shaped blooms in shades of pink, orange, purple or white. The spreading or cascading habit suits hanging baskets and window boxes well.

How to grow Diascias like well-drained compost (soil mix), especially in winter, but plentiful moisture in the summer growing period. Add water-retaining gel crystals to hanging baskets. Trim spent flower stems and feed to encourage new flushes. Plants often overwinter in sheltered gardens. Trim away the old flower stems at the beginning of the new season.

Height and spread 25–45 x 45–60cm/10–18 x 18–24in.
Hardiness ✳✳ Zone 5.
Other plants There are many new cultivars but 'Ruby Field', is hardy and flowers through summer and autumn. Also try the aptly named 'Coral Belle' and 'Lilac Belle' and the related *Nemesia* cultivars, which include more blue-purple shades.

Other plants for pots & containers
* **Black-eyed Susan**
  Thunbergia alata
* **Double daisy**
  Bellis perennis
* **Dwarf daffodils**
  Narcissus cyclamineus types
* **Dwarf pincushion flower**
  Scabiosa 'Butterfly Blue' or 'Pink Mist'
* **Fuchsia (bush and trailing)**
  Fuchsia cvs.
* **Lily**
  Lilium American hybrids
* **Mini cyclamen**
  Cyclamen cvs.
* **Nemesia**
  Nemesia Maritana Series
* **Swan River daisy**
  Brachyscome mulitifida and others
* **Winter flowering violas**
  Viola Sorbet Series

Planting to attract wildlife

Poached egg plant/ Douglas' meadowform
Limnanthes douglasii

Nestled close to the ground, this hardy annual makes a big impact with its yellow and white blooms, which attract hoverflies and bees. Plant with other annuals among fruits, vegetables and roses to attract natural predators and help control aphids and other pests.
How to grow This plant self-seeds freely. In spring, sow directly into well-drained, raked soil in full sun. Make repeat sowings later in spring and summer for continuity of flowers. There's no need to deadhead or feed plants.
Height and spread 15 x 15cm/ 6 x 6in.
Hardiness ❋❋❋ Zone 5.
Other plants The species is the best for wildlife.

Cotoneaster
Cotoneaster spp. and cvs.

Members of this genus range from large, sprawling shrubs and small trees to low, dense bushes. Masses of tiny white or sometimes pink-tinged flowers open in spring and early summer and are usually followed by red berries, though some cultivars have yellow, orange-red or pink fruits.

Cotoneasters provide cover and nesting sites for birds, nectar and pollen for insects and fruits for birds and animals.
How to grow In general, they are very tolerant and will grow on quite heavy clay soils and in cold, exposed positions. They prefer sun but tolerate partial shade. Prune lightly in spring – last year's branches and older wood bear the flowers. Dig up unwanted seedlings.
Height and spread 30–300 x 180–300cm/12–120 x 70–120in.
Hardiness ❋❋❋ Zone 4.
Other plants Larger plants include *C. franchetii* and *C. frigidus* 'Cornubia'. For ground cover try *C. salicifolius* 'Gnome' or *C. x suecicus* 'Coral Beauty'. Medium bushy shrubs include *C. conspicuus* 'Decorus' and *C. horizontalis* when not wall-trained.

Purple top verbena/ purple top vervain
Verbena bonariensis

This slightly tender perennial from South America has an exceptionally long flowering period and often continues from midsummer through to late autumn given shelter from frost. It's a magnet for bees and butterflies. The flat or slightly domed heads of tiny purple

blooms are held at the ends of stiff, wiry branches and the whole plant has an upright feel.
How to grow Full sun, well drained soil and a warm sheltered spot can help plants through the winter, but even if they die, you'll often find the little square-stemmed, slightly bristly seedlings in spring and early summer. They rarely need support, though some twiggy sticks pushed into the ground early on will help in windier spots. Easy to grow from seed on a windowsill in spring. Pot on (prick out) and harden off plants before they go into borders.
Height and spread 180 x 60cm/70 x 24in.
Hardiness ❋❋ Zone 7.
Other plants Verbenas are varied and many half-hardy upright and trailing kinds, such as Temari and Tapien Series, are used in containers, and these attract small hoverflies. The upright tender perennial *V. rigida* has violet blooms. It too is popular with bees and butterflies.

Ice plant/stonecrop
Sedum spectabile

This perennial comes into its own in autumn when lots of butterflies and bees zoom

in to its domed heads of tiny flowers. The pink-darkening-to-brownish-red of many cultivars, including 'Indian Chief', works well with other butterfly flowers, such as butterfly bush. The fleshy blue-green leaves and broccoli-like appearance of the flower-buds make this a lovely front-of-border plant.
How to grow It tolerates most soils, including clay ones. It likes full sun but also light shade. Leave the dead heads as these are ornamental well into winter. Tidy old stalks in spring and divide plants every two or three years as otherwise they have a tendency to flop when in bloom.
Height and spread 45 x 45cm/ 18 x 18in.
Hardiness ❋❋❋ Zone 3.
Other plants As well as the pink or white *S. spectabile* cultivars, try the brick pink *S.* 'Herbstfreude' (Autumn Joy) and dark-stemmed *S. telephium* 'Matrona'. Lower-growing sedums, usually called stonecrops, include many excellent insect plants such as the creeping *S. acre*, which has yellow flowers, and pink-flowered 'Vera Jameson' and 'Ruby Glow'.

▲ *Poached egg plant*

▲ *Cotoneaster*

▲ *Purple top verbena*

▲ *Ice plant*

▲ *Butterfly bush*

▲ *Grape hyacinth*

▲ *Sunflower*

▲ *Geranium*

Butterfly bush
Buddleja davidii

In late summer, the tapering, cone-shaped blooms of these quick-growing shrubs are often covered with butterflies feeding on the nectar. Buddleja cultivars are numerous, but all seem to be attractive to insects. They come in shades varying from purples and purple-pinks to white, and look best in mixed borders with herbaceous perennials, roses and other flowering shrubs.

How to grow Grow in well-drained soil in full sun. Plants flower on the current season's growth, which means they can be cut hard back in spring to a low framework of branches. Pruning is a good idea as plants can otherwise get very tall and leggy and don't live as long. Dead flowers provide sanctuary for minibeasts in winter.

Height and spread 180 x 150cm/70 x 60in.
Hardiness ✳✳✳ Zone 5.
Other plants *B. davidii* 'Black Knight' has very deep purple blooms. 'Pink Perfection' has larger than normal rich pink flowers and 'Dartmoor' has purple blooms with many forks, producing an eye-catching display. 'Lochinch' has paler purple flowers, each with an orange 'eye', and silvery green leaves.

Grape hyacinth
Muscari armeniacum

For early butterflies and solitary bees, finding a clump of these rich blue bulbs in flower in spring is a bonus. Although there are numerous ornamental cultivars and species, this grape hyacinth is best for the wild garden, where it spreads to form colonies.

How to grow Plant the small white bulbs in large clusters at least 10 at a time, but don't plant them too close to one another as the bulbs will need space to expand. Any well-drained soil in sun will do. They also work well in shallow pots as a foil for yellow violas and dwarf red tulips.

Height and spread 20 x 30+cm/8 x 12+in.
Hardiness ✳✳✳ Zone 4.
Other plants 'Valerie Finnis' is an ice-blue variety. Avoid the double 'Blue Spike', which isn't useful to insects.

Sunflower
Helianthus annuus

This hardy annual can produce towering plants with giant sun-shaped blooms. Others are smaller, but the disc-shaped centres are still attractive to honey bees. The black seeds provide a feast for finches.

How to grow Start off in individual pots on a warm windowsill in spring or sow directly in the ground where they are to flower. They thrive in well-drained soil and full sun. Large forms may need staking with a bamboo cane (stake). Grow medium or dwarf kinds in pots. Feed and water potted plants in summer.

Height and spread 90–300 x 45–60cm/35–120 x 18–24in.
Hardiness ✳✳✳ Zone 7.
Other plants Avoid doubles such as 'Teddy Bear', which are no good for wildlife. For towering blooms try 'Russian Giant'. 'Music Box' is a compact form with banded blooms in a range of colours.

Cranesbill
Geranium 'Johnson's Blue'

There are several blue cranesbills, but the dish-shaped blooms of 'Johnson's Blue' seem to glow, even in partial shade. Like most blue flowers, this perennial is a favourite with bees, which are attracted by the colour and the nectar guides. It flowers all summer and the foliage makes good ground cover.

How to grow Any fertile soil will do as long as it isn't very dry or waterlogged. Plant in spring or preferably autumn to give plants chance to establish. Tidy spent flower stems after the main show.

Height and spread 45 x 60cm/18 x 24in.
Hardiness ✳✳✳ Zone 4.

Other plants All the single hardy geraniums are good for bees and range from long-flowered alpines, such as *G. cinereum* 'Ballerina', to ground-cover plants, such as the *G.* x *oxonianum* 'Wargrave Pink'. *G. himalayense* have large, purplish-blue blooms and the late-flowered *G. wallichianum* 'Buxton's Variety' is light blue with a large white eye.

Other plants to attract wildlife
✳ **Aster/Michaelmas daisy**
   Aster spp. and cvs.
✳ **Aubrieta**
   Aubrieta
✳ **Balkan scabious/knautia**
   Knautia macedonica 'Melton Pastels'
✳ **Bee balm/bergamot**
   Monarda didyma cvs.
✳ **Bellflower**
   Campanula percisifolia
✳ **Bidens/beggarsticks**
   Bidens ferulifolia
✳ **Black-eyed Susan**
   Rudbeckia fulgida
✳ **Californian poppy**
   Eschscholzia californica
✳ **Catmint/catnip**
   Nepeta x *faassenii*
✳ **Cornflower**
   Centaurea cyanus
✳ **Firethorn**
   Pyracantha
✳ **Tickseed/coreopsis**
   Coreopsis tinctoria

Planting for quick-growing veg and salads

Lettuce
Lactuca sativa
There are two main types of lettuce: ones that make a solid, crisp 'head', and loose-leaf kinds. Loose-leaf ones are better as leaves are picked individually, allowing you to crop over a longer period. Some varieties are suitable as cut-and-come-again baby leaf salads, where the root and base of the plant are left in the ground after cropping, allowing them to regrow for another harvest.

How to grow Start seed off in pots on the windowsill in early spring, ready for planting out after hardening off. When the weather warms up you can sow directly in the ground every couple of weeks to ensure continuous supplies. Cold-hardy varieties allow you to extend the season in cold frames or under cloches. Improve germination in hot weather by making a seed drill (furrow) and watering it before sowing. Watch out for slugs. Improve soils by adding moisture-retentive compost and manure, and water plants in hot summers to prevent 'bolting' (producing flowers).
Height and spread 15–30 x 30–40cm/6–12 x 12–16in.

Hardiness ❋❋ Zone N/A.
Other plants For colour, sow 'Lollo Rossa' types with red frilly leaves, or other red-leaved types such as 'Red Salad Bowl'. Mixtures are also sold as cut-and-come-again lettuce. For small, quick heads try 'Little Gem' or 'Tom Thumb'.

Rocket/arugula
Eruca sativa
The spicy salad leaf, rocket, or to give it its Italian name, arugula, is perfect for livening up lettuce or tomato salads and for flavouring pasta dishes, risottos and omelettes. It is an incredibly easy summer crop to grow outdoors and, once it is in the garden, it tends to seed around.

How to grow Sow this hardy annual under cover in early spring or autumn, in a cold frame or under cloches (hot caps). Sow directly outdoors as soon as you can prepare a well-raked seedbed in mid- to late spring. Make sowings every couple of weeks. Avoid sowing on ground previously used for brassicas, such as cabbage, as rocket is closely related and land needs to recover for two years to avoid disease build-up. Neutral to alkaline soils are best. Keep well watered to prevent it from bolting (producing flowers) in hot weather. Pick whole young plants (they will re-sprout from a basal stump) or young leaves. Protect against flea beetle using horticultural fleece.
Height and spread 30 x 30cm/ 12 x 12in.
Hardiness ❋ Zone N/A.
Other plants 'Apollo' and 'Skyrocket' are good varieties. Wild rocket has stronger-flavoured leaves.

Radicchio
Cichorium intybus
The deep red radicchio leaves, with their prominent white veins, make this one of the most attractive-looking vegetables to use for salad leaves. The flavour becomes more bitter with age, so pick sweeter baby leaves in early summer if you don't like the bitter taste, or mix just a few with salad leaves, such as lettuce, to add a sweet note. Try brushing leaves with olive oil and baking them in the oven for a side dish.

How to grow For early pickings of baby leaves, sow directly in the ground in mid-spring in shallow, pre-watered drills. For a later autumn crop, which will survive light frosts, sow again in midsummer. Or, sow every three weeks for continuity.
Height and spread 30 x 30cm/ 12 x 12in.
Hardiness ❋❋ Zone N/A.
Other plants 'Treviso Precoce Mesola' and 'Palla Rossa' are attractive and yummy.

Cress
Lepidium sativum
One of the fastest salads to grow, tasty cress seedlings can even be raised on moist kitchen paper on a windowsill in winter, ready for cropping in a week!

How to grow Sprinkle seed on the surface of any moist growing surface, including seed or potting compost (soil mix). Water and cover pots or trays with a plastic bag and stand in a warm place with some indirect light. Once the seed germinates, take off the bag and move to a spot with better light. Keep moist. Crop using scissors. Also sow directly in the soil outdoors between crops in summer.
Height and spread 5–7.5 x 1cm/2–3 x ½in.
Hardiness ❋❋❋ Zone N/A.
Other plants Common, broad-leaf or curled cress (such as 'Extra Double Curled')

▲ *Lollo Rossa lettuce*

▲ *Rocket*

▲ *Radicchio*

▲ *Cress*

▲ *Salad onion*

▲ *Radish*

▲ *Carrot*

▲ *Sweetcorn seedlings*

has a peppery flavour. In supermarkets you usually find boxes of seedlings marked 'cress' that are mainly grown from the milder flavoured rape seed. Mustard seed can substitute for cress too.

Salad onion/scallion
Allium cepa
Salad onions (also called spring or bunching onions) are useful for sowing in gaps where slow-maturing crops have been harvested, as well as in patio containers filled with loam-based potting compost (soil mix). They are ready for harvesting in three months and you eat both the leaves and the swollen stem base.
How to grow Sow from early spring to midsummer in short rows 13mm/½in deep. Thinning out seedlings isn't really necessary. Repeat sowings every three weeks to keep you supplied with plants throughout the summer and into autumn. Late summer sowings using a hardy variety will produce a spring crop.
Height and spread 30–45 x 30cm/12–18 x 12in.
Hardiness ✳✳ Zone N/A.
Other plants *Allium cepa* 'North Holland Blood Red' is dual purpose – use thinnings for salad onions and leave the rest to mature as red maincrop onions. 'Lilia' is also dual purpose. 'Summer Isle'

and 'White Lisbon' are mild-tasting. 'Guardsman' is easy and reliable as it is resistant to frost and disease.

Radish
Raphanus sativus
This mustard family plant has crisp, juicy roots with a peppery tang. It is an annual and is quick and easy to grow. Crop the round- or cylinder-shaped roots when small and tender, as large, old radishes go woody and are more strong-tasting.
How to grow Sow every two or three weeks from mid-spring. Keep well watered and shaded from strong sun. In pots, grow in a loam-based compost (soil mix) with added slow-release fertilizer granules. Watch out for cabbage caterpillars and flea beetles. Protect sowings with horticultural fleece (floating row covers).
Height and spread 6–7.5 x 5–7½cm/2½–3 x 2–3in.
Hardiness ✳ Zone N/A.
Other plants Grow 'Cherry Belle', 'French Breakfast' (cylindrical) and 'Jolly' for a long season and mild flavour.

Carrot
Daucus carota
Growing your own mini carrots is easy and it is very satisfying to pull bunches from the ground with their leaves intact. Look out for round varieties and unusually coloured types.

How to grow For ease of growth, go for quick-maturing, short or round carrots for summer and early autumn cropping, as these don't mind less-than-perfect soil and can be grown in tubs. Sow thinly in short drills (furrows) directly where they are to grow. To protect carrots in the ground from carrot root fly, use a barrier of horticultural fleece (floating row cover) held up with canes (stakes).
Height and spread 18–25 x 20cm/7–10 x 8in.
Hardiness ✳✳✳ Zone N/A.
Other plants Try the quick-cropping round 'Parmex' or cyclindrical 'Amsterdam Forcing'. 'Ideal' is good for baby carrots. 'Purple Haze' is purple on the outside!

Sweetcorn
Zea mays
You can grow sweet cobs even in poor summers. Super-sweet varieties are bred for – you guessed it – extra sweetness. Pick, cook and eat cobs straight away for the best flavour.
How to grow Start off seed in mid-spring by sowing in peat or fibre pots (to avoid root disturbance) on a warm windowsill. Pot on (prick out) and plant out when danger of frost has passed. Choose a sunny, sheltered spot. Prepare the soil well, digging in plenty of manure and applying slow-

release fertilizer. Cover the soil with black plastic or cloches (hot caps) for a few weeks to warm soil before planting out seedlings. Plants are pollinated by wind and produce better crops when grown in blocks. Tap the male flowers or tassels in midsummer to encourage pollination. Feed plants with liquid fertilizer when cobs start to swell. Keep well watered.
Height and spread 150–230 x 25cm/60–90 x 10in.
Hardiness ✳ Zone N/A.
Other plants 'Sweetie Pie' and 'Lark' are sweet and juicy with a soft texture.

Other quick veg and salads
* **Baby leeks**
  Allium ampeloprasum porrum
* **Lamb's lettuce/ mâche**
  Valerianella locusta
* **Mizuna**
  Brassica rapa var. *nipposinica*
* **Pak choi/bok choy**
  Brassica rapa chinensis
* **Pea shoots**
  Pisum sativum
* **Spinach**
  Spinacea oleracea
* **Spinach beet**
  Beta vulgaris
* **Watercress**
  Nasturtium officinale

Planting for slower-growing veg

Sweet pepper
Capsicum annuum var. annuum

These tender members of the potato family, closely related to hot chilli peppers, need a long growing season to produce their fruits. Given the chance to ripen, peppers turn from more strongly flavoured green peppers to sweeter yellow, orange or red fruits.

How to grow Sow seed in individual pots in a heated propagator in early spring and pot on (prick out) as they grow, providing warmth and lots of light. Or, buy seedlings or young plants. Harden off and plant out after all risk of frost has passed and grow in grow bags or large pots on a sunny, sheltered patio. Support with small stakes and soft twine. Water regularly and feed with tomato fertilizer when fruits begin to form.

Height and spread 30–65 x 23–40cm/12–26 x 9–16in.
Hardiness ✴ Zone N/A.
Other plants The dwarf variety 'Redskin' is ideal for pots.

Tomato
Lycopersicon esculentum

No sunny patio should be without a few pots or grow bags of tomatoes and these productive plants provide sweet, juicy treats through from midsummer until autumn.

How to grow Sow in a warm, light place in early spring, covering with clear plastic, or use a propagator. Seedlings must have good light to grow strongly. Alternatively, buy sturdy plants with dark green leaves. Pot on (prick out) and plant out after all risk of frost has passed in individual 25cm/10in pots or grow bags. Hanging, tumbling and dwarf bush varieties are ideal for baskets and troughs (see page 235). Feed with liquid tomato fertilizer when flowers appear and keep well watered. Pinch out side shoots of cordon varieties when they are about 2.5cm/1in long. When plants have produced four fruit clusters, pinch out the growing point a little way above the tomatoes so that fruits have a chance to ripen. Stake cordon varieties with canes and twine.

Height and spread 45–90 x 45cm/18–36 x 18in.
Hardiness ✴ Zone N/A.
Other plants Cherry fruited cordon types include the red coloured 'Sweet 100', 'Gardener's Delight' and the yellow 'Sungold'.

Squash
Cucurbita pepo/ C. moschata/C. maxima

The so-called winter squashes, including pear-shaped butternut squash and round pumpkin lookalikes, are harvested in autumn and the skin left to harden in the sun, allowing the fruits to be stored. Summer squashes are more like courgettes and include patty pan squashes, which look like mini flying saucers. These are cropped during the growing season when the skin is soft.

How to grow Sow one seed to a pot on the windowsill in late spring and cover with a plastic bag. Remove the bag when the seeds germinate and pot on (prick out) as needed. Harden off and set out after all risk of frost has passed. Some are bush types, which need no support, and others are trailers, which can be coaxed to climb up a sturdy frame – check the packet for instructions. Add manure to the ground and water well during the growing season. All make large sprawling plants so make sure you leave enough room.

Height and spread 45–90 x 90–400cm/18–36 x 36–160in.
Hardiness ✴ Zone N/A.
Other plants Try 'Sunburst' F1 (patty pan type) or the squash 'Baby Bear', which produces small orange pumpkins.

Cucumber
Cucumis sativus

This tender salad vegetable is most often grown as a climbing plant in a greenhouse or in large cold frames. Some compact, bushy varieties are ideal for grow bags or 25cm/10in pots on the patio. Choose a warm, sheltered, sunny spot. The fruits of these are quite small, sweet and juicy. Peel those with prickly skins.

How to grow Raise plants on a warm windowsill in spring, planting the large, flat seed on edge. Cover the pots with plastic bags. The young plants have large leaves and grow quickly but can't be put outdoors until warm nights (16–24°C/60–75°F) are ensured. Use loam-based potting compost (soil mix) with added granular fertilizer. Water with liquid tomato food when flowers form. Pick fruits regularly.

Height and spread 60–90 x 90cm/24–36 x 36in.
Hardiness ✴ Zone N/A.
Other plants Rocky F1 and Zeina F1.

▲ *Sweet pepper*

▲ *Cherry tomato*

▲ *Squash*

▲ *Cucumber*

▲ *Yellow courgette*

▲ *French bean*

▲ *Oregon sugar pod pea*

▲ *Beetroot*

Courgette/zucchini
Cucurbita pepo

A tender but quick-growing summer vegetable, the courgette is productive and you should only need one or two of these large plants to keep you supplied with courgettes from midsummer through until autumn.

How to grow Young plants are readily available from garden centres in late spring and early summer, but you can also sow in pots on a warm windowsill throughout spring. Pot on (prick out) and harden off gradually and don't plant out until all risk of frost has passed. Plants require humus-rich soil with plenty of manure to thrive. Water during dry spells.

Height and spread 30–60 x 120–160cm/12–24 x 45–62.5in.

Hardiness ❋ Zone N/A.

Other plants Grow green or yellow cylindrical- or ball-shaped varieties, such as 'One Ball F1' or 'Tristar'.

Runner/pole and dwarf/bush beans
Phaseolus coccineus/ P. vulgaris

Unlike hardy broad (fava) beans, these tender climbers can't be planted out until all risk of frost has passed. The large, heart-shaped leaves and colourful pea flower blooms make runner beans attractive plants for large containers on the patio, growing up cane wigwams. Dwarf bushy French beans need minimal staking. Pollinated mainly by bumble-bees, bean pods are produced for a long period.

How to grow Start beans off in pots on a warm windowsill in early to mid-spring. Plant out after plants are hardened off and all risk of frost has passed. Protect early sowings with cloches (hot caps) and pre-warm the soil with black plastic. You can also sow directly in the ground. Prepare soil thoroughly beforehand. Water plants well when in flower and fruiting. Pick often to encourage more beans to grow. Don't eat raw pods.

Height and spread 45–180 x 40–50cm/18–70 x 16–20in.

Hardiness ❋ Zone N/A.

Other plants The dwarf runner bean 'Hestia' is good in patio pots. The dwarf green bean 'Purple Teepee' has attractive purple pods.

Mangetout/snow peas and snap peas
Pisum sativum

Unlike maincrop garden peas, mangetout and snap peas are easy to grow. The sweet, crunchy pods of snap varieties are irresistible eaten raw or lightly cooked. Mangetout types contain embryonic peas and are flatter than some snap peas, but are cooked in the same way.

How to grow They are best sown into soil that has been warmed up in early spring with black plastic. For early crops, sow in peat pots or modular trays on a windowsill. Plant out as soon as shoots appear and protect with horticultural fleece (floating row cover) or cloches (hot caps). Prepare the ground by digging in manure. Most varieties need support in the form of twiggy pea sticks or a frame of canes (stakes) covered in fine netting. Make a repeat sowing in late summer for an autumn crop.

Height and spread 45–90 x 45–180cm/16–35 x 16–70in.

Hardiness ❋ Zone N/A.

Other plants 'Sugar Ann' is a dwarf, podded snap pea that doesn't need staking. 'Oregon Sugar Pod' is a taller mangetout type.

Beetroot/beet
Beta vulgaris

Very easy to grow, you can harvest sweet little baby beetroot in only seven weeks for use in a range of dishes. The dark, handsome leaves are red-veined and can be picked young for salads or steamed lightly.

How to grow Sow seeds directly in fertile soil using a bolt-resistant variety if you are sowing in early spring, under cloches (hot caps). Add a granular fertilizer containing plenty of nitrogen. Keep the plants well watered. Make repeat sowings until midsummer for a steady supply of baby beetroot.

Height and spread 30–40 x 25–16cm/12–16 x 10in.

Hardiness ❋❋❋ Zone N/A.

Other plants 'Boltardy' is ideal for early sowings. 'Pablo' is a good variety for patio pots.

Other long-cropping veg

- ❋ **Aubergine/eggplant 'Baby Rosanna'** *Solanum melongena*
- ❋ **Broad bean/fava bean** *Vicia faba*
- ❋ **Cabbage** *Brassica oleracea* form
- ❋ **Curly kale/borecole** *Brassica oleracea* form
- ❋ **Onion/shallots** *Allium cepa/ A. ascalonicum*
- ❋ **Potato** *Solanum tuberosum*
- ❋ **Pumpkin 'Little October'** *Cucurbita pepo* form
- ❋ **Purple sprouting broccoli** *Brassica oleracea* form

Planting for easy-growing fruit

Strawberry
Fragaria X ananassa
You can buy strawberry varieties that fruit in early summer, as well as so-called 'perpetual' or 'ever-bearing' types that may flower at intervals through summer into autumn. Mixing varieties carefully gives a range of fruiting times and flavours. Early strawberries may need their blossoms protecting from spring frosts with cloches (hot caps). Strawberries don't take up much room and you can even grow them in hanging baskets (see page 65).

How to grow Plant in late autumn into well-prepared free-draining soil that has had plenty of manure dug in. With summer-fruiting types, take off the flower stems in the first year to help plants build up a strong root system. When establishing perpetual types, take off the spring flowers but leave the summer ones to develop fruits. Feed with liquid tomato food as fruits start to develop. Avoid watering overhead. Raise fruits off the ground with straw to keep them clean and to deter the main pest – slugs! Take off dead foliage in autumn to minimize disease.

Height and spread 30 x 60cm/12 x 24in.
Hardiness ✳✳✳ Zone 5.
Other plants 'Malling Opal' and 'Aromel' are both 'ever-bearing' types.

Raspberry
Rubus idaeus
These soft, red summer fruits can be worked into any corner of the garden, even lightly shaded areas. They grow best in the ground.

How to grow Plant bare-rooted summer- or autumn-fruiting raspberry canes in late autumn or winter in well-prepared ground with plenty of manure dug in. Attach canes to a support of horizontal wires. Mulch. Feed and water during flowering. Net to protect from birds. Cut fruited canes down to 5cm/2in from ground level, but tie in the paler green new canes to the supports, ready to flower and fruit next year. With autumn-fruiting types, cut all canes back after cropping.

Height and spread 150–200 x 120+cm/60–80 x 45+in.
Hardiness ✳✳✳ Zone 4.
Other plants Try non-bristly stemmed summer raspberries, such as 'Glen Ample' or 'Glen Rosa', or the autumn raspberry 'Autumn Bliss'.

Blackberry
Rubus fruticosus
The large, juicy black fruits of this rose relative are easy to grow and bumble-bees love to forage among the white, dish-shaped blooms. Choose thornless varieties and ones that aren't too vigorous so that you can grow them in large tubs (see pages 68–9) or control their spread by growing in the ground and tying the canes to support wires on a fence. Good varieties fruit from late summer well into autumn.

How to grow Plant bare-rooted canes in late autumn or winter (avoiding frosty periods). They tolerate a wide range of soils but best results come from a sunny spot and well-manured soil. Cut off fruited canes when they have finished cropping, about 5cm/2in above ground level. Allow the new growth (which hasn't fruited) room to expand. Tie these new canes in to supports, bending the stems diagonally or towards the horizontal to stimulate flowering.

Height and spread 90–180 x 120–180cm/35–70 x 45–70in.
Hardiness ✳✳✳ Zone 4.
Other plants 'Loch Ness' and 'Oregon Thornless' are excellent prickle-free varieties.

Blueberry
Vaccinium corymbosum
These ericaceous (acid-loving) shrubs not only have rich autumn leaf tints, but they also produce delicious blue-black berries.

How to grow Even if you don't have the right soil, you can grow blueberries in large pots using ericaceous compost (soil mix) with added loam. Plant several cultivars to improve pollination and fruiting and keep plants well watered when in active growth. See page 67 for further care instructions.

Height and spread 120–180 x 60–120cm/48–70 x 24–48in.
Hardiness ✳✳✳ Zone 5.
Other plants Try 'Blue Crop' and 'Bluetta', but also check with local nurseries for their recommendations.

Gooseberry
Ribes uva-crispa
Though thorny, this delicious summer fruit has a unique flavour. Tart green gooseberries require cooking, but there are also sweet ones that can be eaten raw once fully ripened.

How to grow Plant bushes on well-prepared ground with good drainage, but avoid dry sites. Some shade is tolerated

▲ Strawberry

▲ Raspberry

▲ Blackberry

▲ Blueberry

▲ *Gooseberry*

▲ *Blackcurrant*

▲ *Cherry*

▲ *Dessert apple*

and even advised for some cultivars. Mulch in spring and water well in dry summer periods. Mildew is the most common problem so plant resistant varieties, and watch out for the little gooseberry sawfly caterpillars. Net to protect from birds, if needed. As a *ribes* species, there may be a growing restriction.

Height and spread 100–120 x 120cm/40–45 x 45in.

Hardiness ❋❋❋ Zone 3.

Other plants 'Invicta' is green-fruited with good mildew resistance. 'Pax' is a red-fruited dessert variety with good resistance.

Blackcurrant
Ribes nigrum

The tart summer fruits of blackcurrant add zest to pies and make wonderful jams. Some varieties have extra-large and sweet fruits.

How to grow Plant bushes in well-prepared ground in late autumn/early winter. Plant 5cm/2in below the original planting level to encourage new shoots to form underground. Firm in well. Next, cut down all the shoots to just above ground level. This encourages more shoots to appear but you won't get any fruits. When plants are established, prune lightly in winter, removing some of the oldest stems to near ground

level and thinning out bush centres to allow in more light and air. Mulch in spring and net to protect against birds. As a *ribes* species, there may be a growing restriction.

Height and spread 120 x 120cm/45 x 45in.

Hardiness ❋❋❋ Zone 3.

Other plants 'Ben Sarek' is a compact form that is ideal for small gardens.

Cherry
Prunus avium

Sweet cherries on a dwarfing rootstock, such as Gisela 5, are not hard to grow even in a patio container if in a warm place. Sour or acid cherries such as 'Morello' will grow and ripen against a cool wall.

How to grow Cherries need deep, fertile soil with plenty of manure to thrive. Drape fleece (floating row cover) over early blossom if frost is forecast but remove it during the day for pollinating insects. Plant two or more cherries for cross-pollination or, if you don't have room, plant self-fertile cultivars. Pick the summer fruits before the birds move in or net to protect the crop.

Height and spread 300 x 300cm/120 x 120in.

Hardiness ❋❋❋ Zone 5.

Other plants Self-fertile sweet cherries include 'Stella', 'Lapins' or 'Sunburst'. 'Morello' is also self-fertile.

Apple (dessert)
Malus domestica

Grown on semi-dwarfing rootstock, apples (dessert or cooking varieties) are easy to look after and you can fit several different types into a garden, even making use of patio tubs (*see pages 68–9*). There are scores of cultivars and it is best to talk to your local nursery or garden centre to work out which will do best in your garden. Most apples need another apple or crab apple to pollinate the flowers, so you need ones that bloom at roughly the same time (perhaps your neighbours' gardens have suitable trees?). Apples should belong to the same pollination group (listed in books and catalogues) or be self-fertile.

How to grow Plant bare-rooted or container-grown trees in early spring. Protect blossom if late frosts are forecast using fleece (floating row cover) at night, but uncover by day to allow bees access. Trees can be free-standing or trained against a wall or fence or on a system of horizontal wires to save space. Avoid hot, dry walls. Prune in summer to reduce the amount of new growth. Water plants in tubs in summer and mulch with manure to help save moisture. Feed as young fruits develop using tomato fertilizer.

Height and spread 160–180 x 90–120cm/65 x 70 x 35–45in.

Hardiness ❋❋❋ Zone 5.

Other plants 'Queen Cox' is a self-fertile cultivar if you only have room for one plant in the garden or on a patio.

Other fruit

❋ **Apple** (cooking)
  Malus domestica
❋ **Cape gooseberry**
  Physalis peruviana
❋ **Cobnut/hazel nut**
  Corylus avellana
❋ **Crab apple**
  Malus cultivars
❋ **Fig**
  Ficus carica
❋ **Grape**
  Vitis vinifera
❋ **Kiwi fruit**
  Actinidia chinensis
❋ **Lemon** (hardier kinds)
  Citrus x *meyeri*
  'Meyer'
❋ **Nectarine**
  Prunus persica var. *nectarina*
❋ **Peach**
  Prunus persica
❋ **Pear**
  Pyrus communis
❋ **Plum**
  Prunus domestica
❋ **Redcurrant**
  Ribes rubrum
❋ **Wild/woodland strawberry**
  Fragaria vesca

Planting for herbs and edible flowers

Basil
Ocimum basilicum
Sweet basil is a half-hardy annual that can be grown in patio pots and grow bags. It makes a great team with tomatoes or in the summer vegetable garden. Pick the leafy shoots, strip off individual leaves and use in a wide range of hot and cold dishes.

How to grow
Buy a pot of supermarket basil, carefully separate out the seedlings and pot up individually. Keep these in a warm, light spot out of direct sunlight until they are established. Pinch out shoot tips to promote bushiness. Alternatively, grow from seed on a warm windowsill in spring, prick out and pot on indoors until it is warm enough outdoors to start hardening them off.

Height and spread 30–45 x 25cm/12–16 x 10in.
Hardiness ✳ Zone N/A.
Other plants There are many different basils and you could end up with quite a collection. 'Genovese' is well-flavoured but also try the pretty purple *O. b. purpurascens* varieties, such as 'Dark Opal' and the frilly 'Purple Ruffles'.

Chives
Allium schoenoprasum
This versatile hardy perennial herb is one of the easiest to grow and will even thrive on heavier soils. Use it to edge beds and borders, allowing the drumstick mauve-pink flowers to come in flushes, or try in pots and window boxes along with other herbs. Cut the leaves with scissors. The flowers are edible and useful for garnishes.

How to grow
Though you can raise plants from seed, the easiest method is to start with a pot of chives or lift a clump from a friend's garden, pull apart small clumps with roots attached, and plant. Avoid dry soils. Clip frequently to encourage new young leaves but leave some plants to flower. Cut back to ground level to rejuvenate plants afterwards. Lift and divide, planting in different parts of the garden to reduce rust disease.

Height and spread 15–25 x 25–30cm/6–10 x 10–12in.
Hardiness ✳✳✳ Zone 3.
Other plants Chinese or garlic chives (*Allium tuberosum*) are larger with white flowers and a more intense onion/garlic flavour.

Parsley
Petroselinum crispum
This versatile, vitamin-packed herb can be added to any number of dishes, used as a garnish, or mixed with other herbs and spices to blend and soften flavours.

How to grow Sow on a windowsill in late winter/early spring. Plant out after hardening off, or sow directly in rows 1.25cm/½in deep in the vegetable plot in early spring and again in early summer (for a winter crop). For ornamental edging, use one of the pretty Moss Curled types. Cut off flower stems and cut leaves frequently. Plants often overwinter.

Height and spread 30–60 x 30–60cm/12–24 x 12–24in.
Hardiness ✳✳✳ Zone 5.
Other plants Flat or plain leaf types, sometimes called French parsley, have more flavour and include 'Gigante d'Italia'. For a frilly Moss Curled type try 'Lissette' or 'Rosette'.

Sage
Salvia officinalis
The strongly flavoured grey-green leaves of sage are used in cooking and are usually combined with other common herbs for general flavouring or for herb stuffings. The blue-purple flowers in early summer are very attractive to bees. Ornamental varieties look great in patio pots and decorative herb/flower baskets, or as border edging.

How to grow Plant in any well-drained soil, including those containing lime, in full sun. Cut old, leggy plants hard back in spring to rejuvenate. Pick young leaves and shoot tips and remove old flower spikes.

Height and spread 45–60 x 90cm/18–24 x 36in.
Hardiness ✳ Zone N/A.
Other plants The yellow variegated *S. o.* 'Icterina' is strong growing and very ornamental. The pink-and-white-splashed 'Tricolor' is pretty but not vigorous. Purple sage *S. o.* 'Purpurascens' has dusty purple foliage.

Coriander
Coriandrum sativum
The parsley-like leaves of this pungent herb are sometimes called cilantro. The seed is even more strongly 'curry' flavoured. It is invaluable for Indian and Thai cooking.

How to grow This hardy annual is best raised directly in a well-prepared seed bed

▲ Basil

▲ Chives

▲ Moss-leaved parsley

▲ Tricolour sage

▲ Coriander

▲ Oregano

▲ Rosemary

▲ Nasturtium

outdoors or in a greenhouse border. Wait until late spring to sow for best results and repeat sowings every few weeks to give continuity of supply. Any well-drained soil will do, but choose a warm, sheltered spot. Cold snaps can cause plants to flower (known as bolting) and die.

Height and spread 30–90 x 30–60cm/12–36 x 24–36in.
Hardiness ✳ Zone N/A.
Other plants For a feathery alternative grown as a cut-and-come-again salad, try 'Confetti'.

Oregano
Origanum vulgare
This important culinary herb, sometimes called wild marjoram, makes low bushy hummocks, topped later in summer with purple flowers that are attractive to bees and butterflies. The small, pungent leaves are invaluable for Mediterranean dishes, such as pizza and pasta, herb butters, breads and omelettes. It is good in patio pots or can be grown as edging in herb and cottage borders.
How to grow Oregano grows in any well-drained soil in full sun. Add grit to compost (soil mix) to improve drainage in patio pots. Creeping/carpeting forms can be divided to increase numbers. Shear off old stems in spring to reveal basal growth of leaves.

Height and spread 30 x 30cm/ 12 x 12in.
Hardiness ✳✳✳ Zone 5.
Other plants 'Aureum' has ornamental golden-yellow leaves and there are also numerous cream or yellow variegated forms of this mint relative. Sweet marjoram (O. marjorana) is grown as a half-hardy annual and has a spicy, pungent flavour.

Rosemary
Rosmarinus officinalis
Brushing past the branches of a rosemary bush releases a pungent aroma from the needle-like leaves. In spring, plants are smothered in small grey-blue flowers – a powerful lure for bees. It is valuable finely chopped or use sprigs to flavour roast potatoes, meats, chicken or barbecued fish.
How to grow This shrubby evergreen herb needs a hot, sunny spot with well-drained soil. It will grow happily even in quite poor or stony ground containing lime. Plants grow quickly and can be trained into short standards for pots or clipped into a loose hedge. Don't prune plants hard back as they may not recover.

Height and spread 150 x 150cm/60 x 60in.
Hardiness ✳✳✳ Zone 6.
Other plants 'Miss Jessopp's Upright' is a popular cultivar with blue-grey flowers, suitable

for hedges or wall training. Other forms may not be as hardy, but are grown for their more vividly blue flowers or trailing habit.

Nasturtium
Tropaeolum majus
The bright orange blooms of traditional hardy annual nasturtiums are peppery tasting and great for livening up a green salad. You can also eat the young, almost circular leaves. Weave in plants between herbs and vegetables or plant to tumble out of hanging baskets. Single, old-fashioned nasturtiums are best for bumble-bees as they have the most nectar.
How to grow Simply push the large seed into planters filled with a well-drained potting compost (soil mix) in spring. The seedlings will come up between plants in hanging baskets and window boxes for a surprise burst of colour. Overfeeding or planting seed on rich, manured soils causes plants to produce all leaf and few flowers and encourages black aphids. Watch out for cabbage caterpillars. Provide pea and bean netting for vigorous climbing nasturtiums.

Height and spread 30–38 x 60+cm/12–15 x 24+in.
Hardiness ✳✳✳ Zone N/A.

Other plants 'Empress of India' has red flowers and dark tinted leaves. 'Alaska' has white marbled leaves and tastes good in green salads. 'Climbing Mixed' grows to 2.4m/8ft.

Other herbs and edible flowers
✳ **Angelica**
  Angelica archangelica
✳ **Bay**
  Laurus nobilis
✳ **Borage**
  Borago officinalis
✳ **Bronze fennel**
  Foeniculum vulgare 'Purpureum'
✳ **Cotton lavender**
  Santolina chamaecyparissus
✳ **Dill**
  Anethum graveolens
✳ **French tarragon**
  Artemisia dracunculus French
✳ **Heartsease**
  Viola tricolor
✳ **Hyssop**
  Hyssopus officinalis
✳ **Lavender**
  Lavandula spp.
✳ **Lovage**
  Levisticum officinale
✳ **Mint**
  Mentha spp.
✳ **Pot marigold**
  Calendula officinalis
✳ **Thyme**
  Thymus spp.

Plant hardiness

Hardiness descriptions

Plant entries in the Plant Profiles section have been given hardiness descriptions, which tell you the minimum temperature difference plants can cope with. You need to know this because if the weather is too cold then the plants may die.

Lots of other things play a part in how a plant will survive. These include altitude, wind exposure, how close to water it is, soil type, the presence of snow or shade, night temperature, and the amount of water received by a plant. So, it is important to check all a plant's requirements before buying it.

Frost tender – may be damaged by temperatures below 5°C/41°F;
✳ **Half hardy** – can withstand temperatures down to 0°C/32°F;
✳✳ **Frost hardy** – can withstand temperatures down to -5°C/23°F;
✳✳✳ **Fully hardy** – can withstand temperatures down to -15°C/5°F.

United States hardiness zones

In the United States the hardiness of plants is given in a different way. The country is divided into zones, shown on the map, and these show the average annual temperature in that area.

As a general rule, if a plant is said to be, say, Zone 4, it will be able to survive in any zone that has higher temperatures, but not in ones that have colder ones. When a range of zones is given for a plant, the smaller number tells you what the coldest temperature the plant can take is, and the higher number tells you how hot it can get before it starts to struggle. These are general guides, however, so do have a look at what plants grow well locally and do some research.

KEY TO ZONES

	Zone 1	Below -46°C (-50°F)
	Zone 2	-46 to -40°C (-50 to -4° F)
	Zone 3	-40 to -34°C (-40 to -30°F)
	Zone 4	-34 to -29°C (-30 to -20°F)
	Zone 5	-29 to -23°C (-20 to -10° F)
	Zone 6	-23 to -18°C (-10 to 0°F)
	Zone 7	-18 to -12°C (0 to 10° F)
	Zone 8	-12 to -7°C (10 to 20° F)
	Zone 9	-7 to -1°C (20 to 30° F)
	Zone 10	-1 to 4°C (30 to 40° F)
	Zone 11	Above 4°C (40° F)

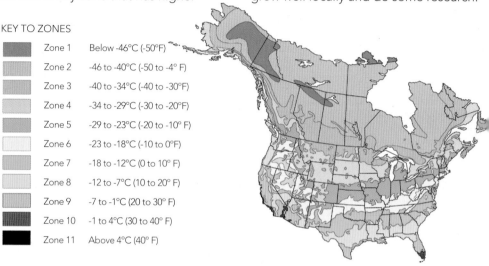

Picture credits

All pictures © Anness Publishing Ltd, apart from the following: t = top; b = bottom; r = right; l = left; c = centre; m = main. **Alamy** 62m, 86cl.

Garden Picture Library 42br, 111tcl, 113tl, 113tr, 115tl, 115tcl, 115tr, 118bl, 119tr, 119tr, 120bl, 120bcr, 120br, 121tl, 121tcl, 121tcr, 121tr.

Garden World Images 112bcl, 113tcl, 115tcr, 118bcr.
iStockphoto 6tr, 8tr, 9tr, 10tr, 12tr, 14tr, 18br, 20tr, 20bc, 20br, 21tr, 21c, 22tr, 28tr, 44br, 46bl, 47m, 52bl, 83tl, 83m, 93tl, 94bl, 96m, 97m, 101tl, 101cl, 104bl, 105bl, 106cl, 110bl, 111tl, 112bl, 118bcl, 118br, 119tl, 120bcl, 122br, 123tl, 123tcl, 123tcr, 123tr, 125tr.
Joanna Lorenz 7bc, 8bc.
Lucy Doncaster 110bcl, 122bl.

Index